*...Forty Years Since
My Last Confession*

WITHDRAWN
No longer the property of the
Boston Public Library.
Sale of this material benefits the Library.

# ...*Forty Years Since My Last Confession*

## A Memoir

*Jean Colgan Gould*

*A Crossroad Book*
The Crossroad Publishing Company
New York

The Crossroad Publishing Company
16 Penn Plaza, 481 Eighth Avenue
New York, NY 10001

Copyright © 2004 by Jean Colgan Gould

All rights reserved. No part of this book may be reproduced, stored in a retrieval system, or transmitted, in any form or by any means, electronic, mechanical, photocopying, recording, or otherwise, without the written permission of The Crossroad Publishing Company.

Printed in the United States of America

**Library of Congress Cataloging-in-Publication Data**
Gould, Jean, 1939-
    Forty years since my last confession : a memoir / Jean Colgan Gould.
        p.   cm.
    ISBN 0-8245-2144-7 (alk. paper)
    1. Gould, Jean, 1939-  2. Catholics – United States – Biography.
3. Ex-church members – Catholic Church – Biography.   I. Title.
BX4705.G617473A3 2004
282'.092–dc22

                                                            2003023304

1  2  3  4  5  6  7  8  9  10        10  09  08  07  06  05  04

*To Irving*

*I would be true*
*for there are those who trust me.*
*I would be pure*
*for there are those who care.*
*I would be strong*
*for there is much to suffer.*
*I would be brave*
*for there is much to dare.*

—*J. Yates Peak*

# CONTENTS

9

### Part III
### PRACTICE

# ACKNOWLEDGMENTS

I N ADDITION TO those specifically named in the following pages, the generosity, wit, and perspective of many others supported me in this project. Initial readers Bill Barry, Nancy Faulkner, and Leslie Miller offered thoughtful comments that determined the book's direction. Sister Maureen Casey and Father Michael Ciccone welcomed my participation in the sabbatical program at St. Stephen Priory. Others who listened patiently to my story as it took shape include Jeannette Atkinson, Marilyn Gardner, Florence Gaylin, Gladys McKinnon, Eleanor Saunders, and Evelyn Wolfson. I am grateful to all.

My editor at Crossroad, John Jones, shepherded me through the publishing process with enthusiasm, respect, and experience. I could hope for nothing more.

Writers often go where those who love them cannot or do not choose to go. I have been particularly grateful for the support of my family during my endeavors to return to Catholicism these recent years. Stephen Pope often knew just the right questions to ask. Deb Colgan and Irving Gould cheered me on, as always.

## ~ Introduction ~

# MY FATHER MYSELF

M Y FATHER USED TO SAY that the details of Catholicism were inconsequential. I remember the word because of the way the syllables stuck in his mouth and because it usually ended my parents' numerous conversations about religion. *Conseeqwenshall.* Before memorizing "the truth" from my school catechism, I imagined a grand kingdom ruled by the remarkably beautiful Lady Novena and a mysterious king called Commander Mint.

When I decided to reconsider Catholicism after a forty-year absence from active practice, my father and his remarks about detail were the scaffolding that held me as I teetered back and forth in my engagement with the modern church. I had no sense then of just how intertwined they were. I was twelve years old when my father died. Though he had been ill for many years and his death was expected, I could not quite believe he was gone forever. A year later my mother sent me away to a Quaker boarding school and my romance with the Catholic Church ended.

When I think of him now, the image of his long, thin frame folding itself at sharp angles into the rose-colored armchair in the corner of our Philadelphia living room comes to me without effort. The cigarette with its decrepit ash dangles from his fingers like a tired Christmas ornament. My mother said he was an impulsive man who defied convention. Perhaps it was the same quality that gave me license to chart the frequently unruly course that became my own life.

He was born in 1900 on a farm in the Illinois prairie to Irish parents, the only son to survive childhood. My father's people groomed him for the priesthood, naming him after the man who was pope just then, Leo XIII. He dropped out of the seminary after two years and escaped to Chicago, finishing his education at Northwestern University. His parents refused to support this enterprise, and he managed by living in a mortuary where he received corpses during the night after the mortician had gone home, a ghoulish detail that attests to my father's determination to gain his freedom. Once he worked as a bill collector, although when a creditor drew a gun against him he vowed never to take such a job again. These were the tales of defiance he enjoyed. Apparently, my father intended to be neither farmer nor cleric.

Yet his religious life, even as a layman, was orthodox in the manner of the times. He attended Mass daily, gave money to the church, and invited priests to Sunday dinner. He insisted that my sister and I attend Catholic school. When he proclaimed the details of the magisterium unimportant, I think he meant that concrete explanations mattered little in questions of faith. If you believed, you accepted the church as truth and light and promise as well as salvation.

In the days of my childhood just after World War II, the Catholic Mass offered a quiet period for reflection and prayer. Parishioners arrived on time, followed the priest in the liturgy with missals, or said their rosaries in silence, perhaps moving their lips to the Hail Mary. If a person coughed or sneezed, it was as softly as possible in a handkerchief so as not to

draw attention away from events at the altar. Both children
and adults folded their hands with fingertips pointing skyward
in prolonged reverence. Served by two altar boys whose crisply
ironed outfits smacked of starch, the priest murmured the liturgy with his back to the congregation. All of us knew the
Latin and its translation, if not from school then from our
missals. We knew when and why bells sounded, when to sit or
stand, and that after every Mass the congregation would kneel
to say three Hail Marys. It was the longest running drama in
history. On any Sunday in any Catholic church in the world,
the ritual was identical. Priests everywhere led the laity in the
same sacrifice of the Mass without variation.

---

*A person can need a long stillness to claim herself.*

---

I missed the comfort of that kind of certainty when I returned to church services. American English came harsh to
the ear after the musical s-sounds of the Latin I had loved as
a child. "The Lord be with you" seemed somehow less than
"Dominus vobiscum" in its quality and depth. Perhaps, I rea-
soned, the alteration of language was an inconsequential detail.
What would my father have thought of the changes? I supposed that faith superseded language and that I was just being
ornery.

My perspective after such a long time away made me both
appreciative and critical. I was, for example, delighted with the
inclusion of music and congregational singing. The fact that
the celebrant created a circle of worship by facing parishioners
made the rite less secretive. But sometimes at the end of Mass

I found myself irritated and confused. The churches reverberated with children and conversation. In an effort to appear more human, priests sometimes spoke too much about their personal lives, or their homilies were uninspiring, even canned. Each liturgy was so different from every other that I got lost in words I had once known by heart and their replacements.

Nothing stays the same, of course. I discovered that church liturgy had been transformed from private prayer to community building. Still, as gentle a gesture as it was, the handshake of peace bothered me as a kind of sixties window dressing. The blend of awkwardness and familiarity had me reeling. From church to church, Mass to Mass, priest to priest — eventually from Catholic to Catholic — I struggled to figure out where and if I belonged. I traveled from Massachusetts to Florida, to Pennsylvania, to Illinois, and back. It sometimes seemed as if I were caught in a children's dot-to-dot game. I wished it were that simple. Only the same gray men appeared everywhere to take up the collection with their long-armed baskets lined with green felt. There was no question: I knew I had, as they say, "come home." But my awakening to the dis-ease inherent in the modern church ate away at the comfort of my renewal.

I did not like to think of myself as shallow. Obviously Catholicism was more than its liturgy. Weightier topics existed that the church had failed to address adequately: birth control, abortion, divorce, women priests, married clergy, homosexuality. Nonetheless, as I tried to find a place for myself it was the details that bothered me most.

The body of Christ had once been so sacred that only the priest could touch it with his fingers. Communicants knelt at the altar railing and closed their eyes as the wafer was placed on their tongues. Returning to their pews, they opened themselves to the infusion of the Lord's grace as the host dissolved in their mouths. A good child would never, never let it touch her lips or her teeth, the Sisters of Mercy told us. Even when the bread and wine were elevated, only a brief glimpse had been permitted. *Sanctus. Sanctus. Sanctus.* Holy. Holy. Holy. When we heard the *Domine non sum dignus,* we beat our breasts three times with closed fists and believed the prayer — that we were truly not worthy.

Today nearly 80 percent of Catholics regard transubstantiation — the changing of bread and wine into the actual body and blood of Jesus Christ, the central act of the Mass — to be symbolic. They receive the host in their hands from Eucharistic ministers, place it in their own mouths, and chew as if it were an ordinary piece of toast. The chomping by the priest himself, amplified by microphone, assaulted my sensibilities and came to represent all that grated on me about the new forms of worship.

*Home. Coming home.* These words imply a physical place rather than a concept of being or way of living. I think that fooled me for a time. From liturgy to liturgy, I resembled a theater critic more than anything else. I reviewed the music, the behavior of the congregation, the homily, the comfort of the seating, the noise of so many churches I lost track.

One Sunday two years after my return, I attended Mass at a church in which the usual holy water fonts at the entryway were replaced with what appeared to be a sizable glass fish tank in the center aisle. Instead of fingertips, my entire hand splashed into the liquid. I snickered. The church was freer with its water these days, frequently reenacting the baptismal ritual. I thought of the great Commander Mint and the lovely Lady Novena of my earliest memories. I thought of my father's prayerful hands in his casket. Most of today's faithful had probably never heard of a novena. Friday fish, ember days, overnight fasting — these and other practices were as dead as my father in his Illinois grave. The "thou-shalt-not" commandments were overlaid by what was called "the love command." I crossed myself with the surplus of holy water. In this environmental age, surely all water was holy. The challenge to decipher what mattered from what was inconsequential remained but had receded.

Why I warmed to the task when so many Catholics had left the church, when I was sixty years old and had lived an entire life already, when those who remained frequently raged at the hierarchy, and when I, more times than not, found myself in radical disagreement with church politics — these are questions that are not entirely answerable. No angel swooped down from on high with wise words. No bells rang. A person can need a long stillness to claim herself. It came as an astonishing simplicity when I once again identified myself as a Catholic — not so much to others as to myself — because, in fact, I had been no other.

*Part I*

# GOOD AND EVIL

# ~ 1 ~

# SEPARATION

**M**Y MOTHER SENT ME TO THE QUAKERS "to be neutralized." This was what she told me many years after the fact. I think it was my father she had hoped — and failed — to alter. She had grown up in inner-city Chicago in an impoverished family with no religious affiliation and been baptized in the church in order to marry him. It was only in her old age that her anti-Catholic views emerged, and she claimed that neither he nor his family had ever accepted her. I was stunned to learn of her bitterness, but it would be wrong to cast her as the villain in this story. She had, after all, raised money for the church while my father was alive. She had never said a word against him. When she chose a Quaker school for me, I think she believed it was necessary to broaden my experience and did not consciously intend to separate me from my faith.

But the opportunity to attend Mass did not exist at my new school. I suppose that I could have left the campus, sought out a church, and insisted on an association with what was then still called "the one true religion." I weighed seventy pounds. The shift from a convent school where children curtsied and committed lists of sins to memory to one that dwelled on an undefined "inner light" but not the teachings of Christ must have been overwhelming. Quaker meetings for worship, held twice weekly, required students to remain in utter silence. Six or eight adults sat opposite us in straight chairs — the "facing bench" — and occasionally spoke, though God was never mentioned. Squirming through these hours, we kids imagined our keepers bald. We gave them medical diagnoses: constipation or dropsy. Compared to the elaborate Catholic ritual, the meetings were without identifiable character. I was unused to religious democracy. Nevertheless, it was easier to abandon the church than to call attention to myself by being different. And if the Society of Friends offered little in the way of traditional religious inspiration, it was rich in its commitment to the welfare of others. Many of the faculty were European refugees brought to the United States by the American Friends Service Committee. Students themselves came from a wide range of backgrounds. I was not unhappy. The campus had a farm among its rolling hills. We built rafts to sail down the local creek. I worked on my tennis game. If I refused to do my homework, nothing happened. Occasionally we hitchhiked into the city. Still, at night I prayed the rosary on my fingertips automatically. In the end, my Catholic training about the requirements of the soul merged with Quaker notions of social conscience to propel me far from the conventional life either of my parents might have imagined for me.

It is not an easy thing to sort out why one person wanders away from active religious participation and another does not. Occasionally during my later schooling when I thought about it at all, I recalled the episode just before the crucifixion where Peter denies Christ, and I wondered if I, too, lacked the courage of conviction. Yet if I'd had to offer an explanation then, I think I might have said that religion belonged to childhood. I was four years old when I began the first grade. Because my father was so ill and I occasionally boarded at the convent, the sisters were especially kind to me. I missed the constancy of their affection after I left them and my childhood behind. In adulthood I would tout them as successful models of alternative roles for women. I would say that whatever I had learned of any value — meaning a love of language and disciplined thought — came from my early days among them. Such statements were couched in the inspiration of their singular lives, of course. As a child, I failed totally in obedience, and I associated chastity with cleanliness. But the notion that one could take a vow of poverty offered relief even then to the inequities I perceived around me. I grew up promising to own only what I could carry and regretting the burden of possessions.

---

*Attending the rituals of believers, even as an outsider, nourished a longing I was unable to identify then.*

---

At twenty-five I briefly wondered how I might return to the church, but the mechanics of it eluded me. Newly divorced with an infant, I had lost touch with the rules. I had not married in the church. My child had not been baptized. What would that mean? I lacked the ability to phrase the questions. Besides, I had no reason to believe I would be welcome. Though my daughter was accepted at a Catholic school for kindergarten, the principal shook her head sadly when I said I had left the church. I retreated to the Friends Meeting in Cambridge, did draft counseling, and protested the Vietnam War.

An aging aunt, my godmother in Illinois, counseled me several years after Vatican II. "Find a nice priest," she said. "Look for a nice older priest, not one of those young ones." She had lived most of her eighty-plus years on a farm not far from the family homestead and then briefly in a Catholic retirement home in Peoria. I was not to see her again.

I played out the scene. I imagined going to confession and admitting it had been years since the last one. I imagined examining my conscience, listing my various sins: venial and mortal. It would be impossible. I considered the penance: two million Hail Marys, three million Our Fathers. It was too late.

At the beginning of my first novel, the protagonist finds herself in a church confessional. "It has been twenty years since my last confession," she says. The priest sounds pleasant, possibly not even punitive. "Yes, my child," he says. But the woman is unable to continue. She sticks her chewing gum on the wall. She runs. It is summer. Thirsty, she drinks holy water from the font by the door. She leaves her sandals in the church.

I couldn't even keep an imaginary character in the Catholic Church. How did I expect a fit for myself?

My father used to take me to his office on Saturdays before illness precluded his working. There he regularly gave an envelope of cash to one Mary McGinty, a widowed cleaning woman with four boys. At the convent we brought our outgrown clothing for the Jewish refugee children who lived among us. The Friends took us to city slums on weekends to clean and paint houses. That any of these was a lesson in religious practice eluded me then. Yet each wove itself into the fabric of my concern about suffering and economics and action — not that I ever did anything in particular to alleviate anyone's pain. I wondered and observed. I wrote. I finished school and began teaching. I remarried. For some years I worked in mental health. None of these things translated into formal religious practice.

During the first year of my high school stint with the Quakers, I began a lifelong fascination with mountain people. Sherpa Tenzing Norgay reached the Everest summit that spring with Edmund Hillary, and even at our remote school in the country we heard about the feat. I was drawn to the Sherpas. Maybe it was the rosy, high cheekbones beneath the dark eyes of these Tibetan traders. Some wore animal skins and trod over snowy mountain trails shoeless. Perhaps I identified with their status as exiles. No doubt I longed for more adventure than my existence as a ninth grader provided.

In middle age I came into a bit of money and used it to go abroad. I returned again and again to the Himalaya to wander through villages where beauty, warmth, and hospitality quite captured me. Without running water, electricity, or more than one set of clothes, and often with only one meal a day, the people had much to teach me about their simple acceptance of the necessity to live with nature rather than to conquer it.

Though traditional Buddhist ceremonies with drums and long horns were foreign to me, attending the rituals of believers, even as an outsider, nourished a longing I was unable to identify then. The Buddhist principle of unity of all living things articulated my own views. When I woke to the chanting of children at a mountain school, or of monks at a monastery, or to the baritone prayers of a favorite guide, I believed myself safe. Once in a temple in the tiny mountain kingdom of Bhutan, sitting cross-legged on a cold stone floor while a lama intoned a blessing, I moved into an expanded moment far from the earth where I witnessed the globe itself spinning with all its suffering and glory. Though I accepted the experience as one of many gifts of the senses at high altitude, it was a strange thing — simultaneously unsettling and affirming — to feel close to God under such circumstances.

But I confess that neither God nor any particular reverence for nature led me to the Andes during the summer of 1999. A powerful curiosity frequently took me away from routine life. The Aymaras in Bolivia worshiped more than one deity as did some eastern Bhutanese. Parts of the mountains in Latin America were said to be very beautiful. I wondered about the similarities among Himalayan and Andean people.

It was my observations of missionaries at work in Bolivia that forced me to take another look at religious practice. At high altitude where illiterate men and women scratched out a living as best they could, a group from southern California, of all places, pressured for the translation of the Bible into Aymaran. On city streets in Sucre, teenagers from Lubbock, Texas, pantomimed the crucifixion. And there were others. At one point I shared a commercial jet with American soldiers in full military gear who were training "the native morons." Each group was so certain of its actions, so patronizing of those they professed to serve. The rigorous and troubling evangelization of indigenous people worked its way into my conscience with a nearly obsessive grip.

I had grown up with stories about missionaries who became saints — men and women who were burned at the stake for their beliefs, people who had their tongues removed for preaching the gospel. Taught sometimes as geography and history rather than religion, the tales made me eager for adventure to foreign lands. They provided the subjects of great art, what the sisters called "Picture Study" at my old convent school, where concentration on the great halos of light muted suffering. More than anything, however, the missionary narratives instituted the first questioning of how far any of us would go to defend our own beliefs or the beliefs of others.

The proselytization, political and religious, I encountered in Bolivia frightened and outraged me with its insensitivity. Do-gooders, I reflected, sometimes act from their own needs. I had done it myself — leapt onto a white horse and rushed off to rescue those who didn't need me in order to feel necessary. You can imagine you are acting from compassion and make things worse. In the Bolivian countryside, I had seen children throw stones at North Americans. When an old Indian man approached and spat at my feet as I sat alone on a park bench one afternoon, I felt responsible for whatever hostility he carried stemming from those he associated with me. But I was unable to know my obligations as a witness.

By chance, I hooked up with a group of Quakers during my final days in La Paz. Among them was a recent alumna of my high school and her parents. One early evening in the plaza just outside the Cathedral of San Francisco, the mother, a gaunt anemic-looking woman, announced that she would never, ever set foot inside a Catholic church. "The papists ruined Latin America," she said. "All that mumbo jumbo. And the statues. Imagine bowing to a statue of Jesus Christ with his heart bleeding. And eating flesh, drinking blood. The religion is barbaric," she said, finally pausing to take a breath beneath her flat bosom. The volume and vituperation of her comments came at me like physical blows. I had seen ugliness before this, but the accumulation of intruders, these many "people of faith," jangled me.

In some perversity of her passion did the Quaker mother's comments push me to defend the church? I was no fan of wealth or colonialism. I did not approve of the Vatican treasures, the ornate robes of the Catholic clergy, the exploitation of peasants to build magnificent houses of worship. I remember that I felt sad for her rage and wondered how she had come to her righteousness. Only among Himalayan Buddhists had I observed universal tolerance for other faiths.

The previous day I had traveled with the Quakers to Suriquiña, a day's journey north of La Paz on the Altiplano, where their group sponsored several projects for indigenous people. There at a rousing church service conducted by the local Quaker pastor, Aymaran women crawled up the aisle weeping, making their bargains with God for food, sober husbands, and healthy children. Several of the visitors photographed the scene. They moved to the front of the tiny church and sang "Oh, God Is Good" in perfect harmony. Afterward they gave out pencils or Life Savers or chewing gum. In August the great plain of rugged grassland had become dry and tired as ashes. Cold winds of great force interrupted the echoes of women's sobs blended with the tones of "Oh, God Is Good." The Quaker mother had led the group in their song with several rehearsals in the minivan. As she wound down her harangue against the Catholic Church, I imagined the small "O" her mouth might form were I to punch her in the solar plexus. That was the thing about ugliness, I thought. It can rub off on you, make you say or do outrageous things. It can make you feel desperate and alone.

The scent of the candle I had just lit in the cathedral to my father's memory lingered. Did I believe that it connected me in some way with the poor souls languishing in purgatory as I had once been taught? I don't think I ever understood the pain of hell or purgatory to be actual fire. Whether they knew it or not, most Catholic kids learned early the differences between figurative and literal language. Ritual provided structure for the faith that held us. In the cathedral that day the several rows of votive candles before me flamed constant in ancient mystery.

The intensity of my Bolivian venture required me to step back, to allow the sensations to course through me over and again. At home I wondered how I would find a context for my questions about "good" people and those whom they "served." What I witnessed was more than right-wing fundamentalism, I decided, more than ugly travelers. It pointed to my own lack of grounding in modern religious thought.

# ~ 2 ~

# SEMINARY

T HE BOSTON THEOLOGICAL INSTITUTE, an umbrella
organization of nine seminaries in the region, listed only
one course in fundamental moral theology available to auditors that fall in its catalogue. That it happened to be given
at a Catholic seminary made no difference to me one way
or the other then, just weeks after my return from Bolivia.
My eagerness to get up to date obscured any denominational
consideration.

So it was that in late September I attended my first class
at the Weston Jesuit School of Theology, nestled within a
few unassuming buildings just blocks from Harvard Square
in Cambridge. The sidewalks shone slick with wet leaves that
afternoon, chilly for autumn. A light drizzle fell. Though the
moisture gave off the sweet scent of summer, the garb of
pedestrians made a contrary statement. Jackets and sweaters
stretched tightly over bodies already beginning to turn as
inward as the Queen Anne's Lace bordering country roads.

I had dressed with great care that day, as if I were going
to a job interview instead of to a class — that is, I wore a
skirt instead of the usual jeans. On finding the correct building, an unexpected awkwardness stiffened my fingers, and my
umbrella jammed as I attempted to close it. Vulnerability was

not a quality I managed with grace. In the jerk of a motion I hid the umbrella behind a shrub like a terrible secret.

When I stepped into the classroom, no one appeared to notice. About thirty men and a dozen women sat on upholstered chairs with wheels, arranged in a semi-circle of three tiers. Long tables served as writing desks. Later I would learn that, as I expected, the majority of students were preparing for the priesthood, though the option to attain graduate degrees drew others already doing pastoral work in their parishes. Several Protestants from other schools had cross-registered. A few nuns and priests on sabbatical programs had also enrolled as auditors. Some were older men considering religious vocations. Nearly one-third were foreign students.

James Keenan, S.J., presided. In a beige crewneck sweater and sports jacket, he could have been any middle-aged man, an insurance salesman maybe, passing on the street. But when he spoke his appearance changed. He became younger, athletic, attractive. His hair was slightly red, hardly gray at all. A Brooklyn accent very nearly required translation. The words galloped from his mouth, connecting all of us with their velocity and intention. Those who knew him from other courses took notes as if the pace was not unusual. The priest's arms and hands dotted phrases, sentences, concepts of importance. He stood in front of the lectern without notes.

I sped to keep up with him. I listened. I wrote. I watched others watching our instructor. It had been a long time since I attempted to adjust myself to another's classroom. I continued writing. I became attuned to the speech pattern. And I understood. It was all too clear that I was caught in a forty-year time warp. Organized religion — Catholicism anyway and maybe Christianity in general — had stood on its head since I had last taken a look at it.

Father Keenan — Jim — spoke several times of "the love command." He spoke of inclusion. "Women and homosexuals need to be welcomed as full participants in the clergy," he said, as if it were necessary to state the dimensions of his political consciousness from the outset.

I wrote "the love command???" on my yellow tablet and quickly covered it with my hand. I had found this course. I had gotten myself to this place. But I was more like a spy than a student. The only commandments I knew began with "Thou shalt not."

The priest was making the case for a "historical" reading of the Bible — now called Scripture. "Its interpretation evolved over time," he said, "and needs to be placed in context for contemporary use."

Well, of course. Catholics had never been literal interpreters of the Bible, had they? In point of fact, they had not been big on the Bible at all. As children, we had learned the Old Testament stories — Daniel in the lions' den, Joseph's coat of many colors, poor Lot's wife — but everyone knew it was the four gospels that counted.

"The focus has shifted," Keenan said, "from lists of sins and evildoing to positive ways of being. The Golden Rule has replaced the Eighth, Ninth and Tenth Commandments."

I ran through the commandments, counting on my fingers to see if I could recite them. I could.

> *Thou shalt not bear false witness against thy neighbor.*
> *Thou shalt not covet thy neighbor's wife.*
> *Thou shalt not covet thy neighbor's goods.*

I wondered if my umbrella was still behind the shrub. I rolled the sound — Love Command — around in my head. I liked it. But could you do that? Could you just change the rules? I guessed that you could. How we had struggled to know the meanings of "false witness" and "covet."

"We'll break for ten minutes," said the priest.

Everyone stood. I got up, too. Some stretched their arms over their heads, and I found myself doing the same thing. Well, good, I thought. I loved the Bible, loved its language and history. I had spent eight weeks for ten years at a Protestant summer camp where each morning the director read from Psalms or Corinthians, using the beautiful language of the King James Version. My college had required a two-semester study of the Old and New Testaments. These would keep me in good stead in this course and in others to follow. I shook my writing hand and introduced myself to the man next to me.

"I guess that sin's no longer in," I said to him. "Is that true?" I could say stupid things, things funny and serious at once, puzzling to listeners, when I was unsure of myself.

"Are you a Catholic or what?" he said, squinting his eyes narrowly.

Well, no, not really. "Oh, yes," I said. *Yes?* "I haven't taken any classes in theology for a long time." I held onto the back of my chair, and its wheels tangled with those of my neighbor.

He never answered my question about sin but mused about the fact that most Catholics no longer took part in the sacrament of reconciliation, which I figured out was the new term for confession. He was an ex-capitalist computer person, he told me, pursuing a doctorate in theology. His square jaw and wrinkled jeans didn't quite match. He was the only student with a laptop.

"I'm a writer," I said.

"I go regularly to confession," he told me. "I mean reconciliation. It's really because of my devotion to the Blessed Mother."

Though I nodded, I had no sense of his meaning. He was thin and long-legged and did not smile easily.

He yawned. "I've got the major responsibility for the care of my elderly parents," he said.

---

### *"Are you a Catholic or what?"*

---

I had recently edited a collection of essays on that very topic. "My mother is ninety," I said, "and living in Florida. It's a no-win situation, isn't it?" I looked at my watch. At four o'clock, my mother would be going down to dinner at the retirement complex where she lived now. The food was terrible, she told me every evening when we spoke. And all her friends were dead. I had hoped by collecting the essays for the anthology that I would learn the things I needed to know about caring for her.

My classmate went on then talking about his family and the demands on his time as he tried to complete his studies at the seminary. "It's a bitch," he said.

His language startled me, but I nodded. Over the years I have learned that I appear especially calm to others when my insides are most wobbly. The day of that first class at the Jesuit seminary I conned even myself until that conversation with Matthew McShane. "Are you a Catholic or what?" When nothing terrible happened, it came to me that I had believed that someone would find me out and bar me from the class.

I was not a practicing Catholic. I had broken nearly all the commandments, though probably not too frequently the love command. If anything, I had loved unwisely and too often. I had been married and divorced and married again. I would never be permitted — I was certain — to attend Mass or take sacraments. Even if I had thought about returning — and I know now that I must have — I was as ineligible as Adam and Eve were to go back to Eden. That day I must have imagined that the skies would grow dark and maybe split open. Maybe even God would descend and wag a long finger at me. But in truth, human ridicule appeared more imminent. I did not want Matthew McShane to find me out.

During the last half of the class, Father Keenan briefly mentioned *Humanae Vitae,* the 1968 papal document that restates the traditional Vatican position disallowing birth control. For a second time he talked about those who look at the scriptures and canon law as fixed. He made another pitch for his own interpretation. "One needs to acknowledge," he said, "that some early ideas are no longer applicable to current times." He was angry, I realized. "Mass, for example, became required on Sundays because it was the only way to reach the peasants who worked seven days a week. The rule was that of man," he said, "a human commandment, not one from God."

Of course. And one of the reasons so many left the church in contemporary times was the refusal of the hierarchy to expand traditional views for modern lives. Apparently, Vatican II showed promise but had ultimately disappointed.

In the 1980s I freelanced for an advertising agency whose major clients were women's Catholic colleges. Struggling with shrinking enrollments, they had lost confidence in the quality of their educational goals. Admissions work had evolved into self-promotion and public relations. I ran focus groups and wrote new materials for prospective students. Many Catholic religious had left their orders, though usually not the church, and continued to teach as laywomen. Sisters who stayed were often equally dissatisfied but chose to work within existing structures to press for progress. Others remained and simply violated the rules. One told me that she had advised students where to go to end their pregnancies, though she drew the line at accompanying them. As I investigated the histories of these institutions and worked on admissions copy with nuns close to my own age, I wondered what had become of the dedicated women who made me feel so safe when I was a child. The Sisters of Mercy had allowed those of us who boarded to slide down the great wooden banister in the lovely old mansion that served as their convent.

The moral theology class ended with student discussion and questions. Concerned hands flew up like small frantic birds after Father Keenan's remarks about the church needing living documents, especially the Bible. He meant to rouse them, I thought, from whatever certainty they brought to his course.

"But," a man wearing a rain hat and long hair spoke, "if we don't have literal interpretation of scripture we have no rules. We have," he paused for effect, "nothing."

Another earnest seminarian in a purple turtleneck threw his palms toward the ceiling with his complaint. "I just don't get it," he said. "Once you know God, why would you walk away?"

"I hate this ethics crap," whispered Matthew, the ex-computer guy sitting next to me. "I'm only interested in scripture." He unplugged his laptop and rolled up the cord in protest.

I wrote his statement in the margin of my notebook. I wondered how a seminarian could care about anything *but* ethics.

Keenan fielded questions with great skill and kindness, challenging each student without talking down to any. "Church doctrine," he said, "is a body full of historical truths continually being understood."

I had once seen a man faint after getting off a plane at an airport situated at twelve thousand feet. The priest's invitation to the class to weigh in by means of theological discourse struck me as a quick infusion of high-altitude air. In my life, I had known only a few teachers whose intellectual brilliance matched their skills in communication and passion.

Outside, after class, the darkening sky glimmered with a handful of early evening stars. One especially young and handsome student sighed as I passed.

"Good night," I said.

"I hope I can do it," he said. "This is going to be my hardest class."

"You'll be okay," I called back to him. "Once you get the lingo, you'll be fine."

The drizzle had stopped. Retrieving my umbrella, I cheered myself aloud. "Oh, good," I whispered. I would never again have to go to the first class at the Jesuit seminary. I sat in my car in its illegal spot and locked the door. Harvard Square belonged now to those who could afford the high rents or to the homeless who congregated at street corners. My first husband and I had spent many hours in the wooden booths of Cronin's Bar & Grill drinking beer and thinking we knew something. Cronin's was as long gone as folk music and marches against war.

When Father Keenan spoke about a progressive reading of the scriptures, he reminded us that Jesus did not sit still. "Did he plant his feet on a hillside and stay there?" he had asked.

"Did he say to stay in this one place in time, in thought, in action? No. He said, 'Rise up and follow me.'"

I was still getting used to the fact that people no longer bowed their heads when they said, "Jesus." But the teacher's words came back to me as I turned on the car engine. It seemed to me that Christian or not, the admonition to keep moving was sound. A certain restlessness had plagued me throughout my life. It had alienated me from cultures that focused on destination, on the bottom line. Like my father, I had never been able to stay in one place for too long. I wished again that I had known him better.

IN THE WEEKS THAT FOLLOWED, my enthusiasm for the moral theology course grew. Occasionally it spilled into my conversations with friends and family, but when their eyes — even some Catholic eyes — glazed over, I usually had sense enough to change the subject. Most human beings were driven more by concrete goals than by ideas.

Eventually, as I hoped, Jim Keenan lectured about those with good motives sometimes making situations worse. "Some people eager to be of service to others have disordered minds," he said. "They ought to stay at home and not interfere."

I remember thinking that most minds were neither ordered nor disordered, but some of each. It was not so easy to know where you stood. Yet the oversimplification didn't matter. Whatever box I had locked myself into over my Bolivian journey had broken apart. Perhaps what I sought all along was personal validation, as well as information and perspective.

Like some of the nuns I'd met in the previous decade, Father Keenan acknowledged his preference to press for change by remaining within the church. "Most institutions are con-servative by nature," he asserted. "As agents of change, the tensions within them are healthy and normal. Controversy can actually be positive."

Some students fidgeted when he said things like this, as if they didn't quite get his point, but it may have been that they had no stomach for conflict. For someone like me, however, who questioned rules, requirements, hierarchical necessity, these remarks arrived as exquisite solace.

I do not want to give the impression that I looked to Jim Keenan as some sort of guru. I didn't. He seemed to me as talented as an Olympic athlete, a gymnast maybe or a skier over a difficult slalom course. I appreciated human excellence. I did not always agree with him, but the wit and energy he brought to the moral theology course gave me hope for a spirit I hadn't known was absent from my life and affirmed what I had held in abeyance.

I had lucked out. If he was representative of where the Catholic Church was at the end of the twentieth century then perhaps I could find a comfortable place within it.

But of course, he wasn't. And I couldn't.

# ~ 3 ~

# PAULIST CENTER

**D**URING THE BEGINNINGS of my thoughts about returning to active Catholicism, I walked around in a kind of weird time machine, frequently getting caught in my attempts to weave forty years of church and personal history into my current life. I began to think that some experiences required new skills, even new language, and I didn't know what they were or how to find them. I often thought of friends whose spelling was so bad that they couldn't find words in the dictionary and understood finally what they meant. I recalled my aunt's advice to find a nice old priest but lacked the imagination to know where I should go. I was afraid. I was afraid of being hurt, though I could not have said so then.

The Franciscans at St. Anthony's Shrine in Boston had published notices for inactive Catholics in the *Boston Globe* some years before this, telling us that we were welcome to come home. Occasionally I sent for information or made a file folder, and then forgetting I had done so began with it all over again. Meetings for alienated Catholics were taking place, the announcement said. It was an opportunity for people to get together and talk about their experiences with the church, including their pain and anger, and possible return. But there was no way I was going to tell my story, whatever it was, to a group of strangers, and I did not want to hear theirs. It was all too personal. I couldn't place myself in such a public setting. The most I could do then was to make a file folder.

It was on the Internet that I found the moral theology course. And it was on the Internet that I discovered the Landings Program at the Paulist Center in Boston.

> The Landings Program provides a safe harbor or landing place for returning Catholics to explore their faith and their future with the Church. Facilitated by active Catholics, the group shares struggles of faith in an accepting atmosphere. The eight-week program concludes with a Saturday retreat.

Clearly it was not very different from the program offered at St. Anthony's Shrine. *I* was different.

In late November, on one of those damp days that promised another bleak New England winter, I made my way downtown to speak with a priest whose last name was Colgan, my father's name, about the possibility of my participation. I rarely got to this part of town anymore and was surprised how little it had changed. Forever in the process of regilding, workers climbed over the gold dome of the State House on Beacon Hill. At the Park Street subway exit, venders hawked plastic replicas of Paul Revere and his horse. An open air trolley of tourists clanged down Boylston Street.

Anxious, I was an hour early. As I walked up Charles Street toward Beacon Hill, the November wind made small howls in the doorways of antique shops. I felt a bead of perspiration in the small of my back. The fear and rush of adrenalin made me a bit high, I thought. I remembered my first class at the seminary. I remembered Bolivia. It was my curiosity that got me in trouble, I decided. I had no capacity for tolerating com-placency. A young painter I knew in Kathmandu had once told

me, "Death is sameness." But constant pursuit of new experience could keep you off balance. Without a clear vision, you
could end up chasing your own tail.

I hummed "Onward Christian Soldiers." Inside the building, a male receptionist turned out to be a former student at
the Weston Jesuit School of Theology. He was a huge man,
a lovely man from Zambia, whose handshake let me know
everything would be as I'd hoped.

When I got off the sixth floor elevator, a man in a
Mr. Rogers cardigan sweater, with just the beginning of a
spreading waistline, greeted me. For a few minutes we tried
to make a family link. The early Colgans had emigrated from
Ireland to Canada and then south to northern Ohio (his family) and to Illinois (my father's people). Oddly his own father
was not a Catholic, he said, despite his name. I wondered if his
father were still living and how he felt about his son becoming
a priest, but I didn't ask.

"I think I want to return to the church," I said. There it was:
the first time I'd said the words aloud, and though I knew I
could renege, the statement felt like a commitment.

Books, macrame wall hangings, and other handmade objects
lined the walls. The chairs were comfortable. If there was a
crucifix I didn't spot it. Did the priest wear a clerical collar? I
think now that he did not. We sat down opposite one another,
and I told him what I thought was my story. Flowered pots of
philodendron perched on the windowsills.

"My father was a devout Catholic," I began. "but he died
when I was twelve."

"How awful for you," said Father Colgan.

For a moment I wondered if this were going to be some kind
of psychotherapy experience, but I went on anyway. I related

the history as I had conceived it — my non-Catholic mother, the Quaker boarding school, my separation from the church, my early divorce. Without warning, the guilt and loneliness I knew had hovered around me for all these years descended, though I did not cry. It had never occurred to me to ask anyone about Mass at my boarding school. Was I to blame then? Should I have insisted I was a Catholic and refused even to attend the Friends school? In those days it was a mortal sin to enter a church of another faith.

The priest nodded. He had listened to maybe hundreds of these stories and knew enough to let me finish without interrupting. And I was grateful that he said nothing, since whatever reactions he might have shared could have closed me down. I had seldom told this story about my father's death and my being sent to boarding school without what I considered an over-reaction from others who led more traditional lives. They meant well, but I felt puny and sometimes wrong as a result of their comments.

Even in today's more psychiatrically informed times, I think it may still be possible to underestimate the impact the surviving parent has on a child. Probably I was afraid my mother would abandon me for good if I argued with her. Her siege with my father's illness had lasted a long time. We had all known he would die eventually. For him, she told me, his death was a blessing. For her, it was a relief. I grieved a long time for the loss I knew about, but was unaware of the magnitude of the separation from my religion.

"So you received no sacraments since that time?"

"That's right," I said, "but I think maybe I never really left the church." I told him about my experience at Weston, how much at home I was there, how pleased I was that it might be possible for me to return since the rules — "they, of course, don't call them rules," I said — had changed. "But I need help with the mechanics."

Two years before this when the concern about my mother's welfare heightened, I had gone to a Mass in Florida, hoping to find extra support for her — not, by the way, from God but possibly from local congregants. I had been trying to manage her care from Boston, spending part of each month there, and I thought a church connection might enable me to broaden my network. I had no conscious plan for any personal Catholic reunion. In the manner of many children of the elderly, I was trying to cover all the bases. Matthew McShane in my class at the seminary was caught up in the same sometimes overwhelming dilemma.

That Mass was excellent preparation for what was to come. I knew about the shift to English and that services were held on Saturday evenings as well as Sunday mornings. But beyond that I knew nothing about the transformation of the liturgy that had shaped my childhood. As I looked now into the broad face of Father Colgan, this man who might be my relative, I recalled the Florida Mass. The whole thing tumbled out as if I could wait no longer to share the experience.

"A sign in block letters on the door said, DO NOT GENU-FLECT," I said. "THE EUCHARIST IS NOT YET PRESENT. The Mass was held in an all-purpose room with block linoleum tiles and metal folding chairs. I sat in the last row. On back of the chair in front of me were more signs with instructions: NO BOOKS ARE USED AT THIS LITURGY. DO NOT SAY THE ROSARY. DO NOT LEAVE EARLY."

My many unfavorable reviews of Catholic Masses had begun. I quite literally did not know how to conduct myself. I had yet to learn what the majority of Catholics already knew: that thirty-five years after Vatican II you still had no idea what you'd get by going to church. It was, in fact, no longer called "going to church."

The altar was a plain table on a platform akin to the stage of a theater in the round. A middle-aged man in khaki shorts lit the candles and served Mass. A young guitarist tuned his instrument before the priest, an old man, entered through the door from which I had come.

"My father often commented that what mattered was faith, not details," I said to Father Colgan.

"He was right," he said.

Okay. So the Holy Spirit had replaced the Holy Ghost. So there were no bells at the Sanctus. And I supposed it was reasonable for the priest to face the congregation. But I had been taken aback when he began talking about himself. He'd had cancer, he told everyone, and radiation. And he was recovering, though we no doubt noticed his weight loss and baldness. This was what he told us even before the Mass began. I was unaware then that Vatican II encouraged priests to become human beings. "I've stopped smoking," the old priest said, "and begun walking." He all but boasted of his conversion to the healthy life. I briefly wondered if he were going to get parishioners to sign up for his health club.

Well, I had only been visiting. Still I questioned the degree of self-revelation, and I said nothing of it now to the Paulist priest. It was only the beginning of my concerns about the personalization of the liturgy. As children, we all knew that priests were human beings. We saw them in our homes, at fund raisers, or in their cars on their way to the golf course. When they knelt facing the altar in the sacristy, we giggled at the holes in the bottoms of their shoes. But they had been servants of the Mass, instruments of the ritual of the Eucharist. It would be much later that I would hear others, even priests themselves, complain about the variations in the service, even within the same church by different celebrants.

But the music that day remains spectacular in my ear. The guitarist gently played and sang responses. He was a lanky teenager with very straight white teeth against his brown cheeks. Even from the back row, I could see that his eyes shone green as the sea.

At least Catholics still got to their feet for the reading of the gospel, after which the priest stumbled through his homily. It had nothing, I was relieved to hear, to do with his cancer. I did not, of course, take communion. My respect for the faith of others kept me an observer. Clearly I was an outsider.

During the entire Mass there were no prayers uttered aloud by the congregation. But at some point, perhaps even before communion, we were instructed to offer each other the sign of peace. Some kissed each other, but most shook hands with those closest to them. Perhaps because it made me more visible than I wished to be then, the exercise struck me as false. It brought home to me, then and later, the fact that there was no longer much, if any, room for private reflection and contemplation at the Catholic Mass.

"I was just so awkward," I said now to Father Colgan. Did I expect him to give me permission? Did I want him to take me to Mass by the hand? Though I was a grown woman, I was aware that a much younger person's emotions were simmering not far from the surface.

"Just go," he told me.

I wondered if he were losing patience with me. "What about confession?" I said. "I haven't been to confession in all this long time."

"Look around you in church," he said, "and do what everyone else does. During the beginning of the Mass, there is a time for self-reflection and examination, a time to ask for forgiveness that can serve for confession."

"There is?"

"And besides, it's called reconciliation now," he reminded me. "And then go up to receive the Eucharist like everyone else."

---

*I did not take communion. My respect for the faith of others kept me an observer.*

---

He made it sound so easy. He had never known the Latin Mass. There would have to be more to it than simply following others. I didn't want to make my reconnection more complicated than necessary, but I knew that renewal would involve a process of getting reacquainted, of balancing knowledge with belief. Like my journeys abroad, conditions and companions could change. Energies could soar or plummet. And in the end, you got through it, of course. But who you were then, afterward, mattered less than how you managed along the way.

"What about the altar facing the congregation?" I didn't know where these questions were coming from now.

"We would never turn our backs on the people," he said as if the very suggestion of it had almost wounded him.

I didn't say anything more. We had been taught that the Mass was an offering to God, not to one another. I must have thought the priest's job was to lead the congregants in that endeavor. After all, he faced the group for the sermon, the homily. Wasn't that enough?

I never said how afraid I was. Probably I didn't need to tell him. He had had others come to him with their stories of regret and hope. But I refused the program of group meetings when I heard they were led by a married couple. Besides, I could never manage an all-day retreat at the end of the eight-week program.

The priest took my questions and comments in stride. He gave me two books he thought might be helpful. The first was a review of Catholic rites as they fit into the calendar year, more of a reference than for any immediate use. The second attempted to place the church as a developing institution in historical context, echoing Father Keenan's views. "Maybe in a year you might want to come back and see me again," he said.

I had a whole shelf of books about Catholicism that I never thought could lead me back from a final excommunication. The "fallen away" appellation seemed designed to make people into sinners. "Lapsed" sounded, if not evil, then deficient. And "inactive" was not much better. I had known the sacraments. I had known what it meant to go without them. I supposed it was a question of knowing what was sinful and what was not, and if I even believed in sin. Did the love command eliminate it or only facilitate forgiveness?

Early on Sunday mornings at my summer camp a small group of us would be taken to Mass across the lake, after which we were required to participate in the Sunday camp service for another hour or two. We all loved the hymns and belted them out in harmony. "Fairest Lord Jesus," "Eternal Father Strong to Save," "Onward Christian Soldiers," "The Battle Hymn of the

Republic," and my favorite, "I Would Be True." I don't think any of us considered it a sin for a Catholic girl to spend her summers with Protestants. For me as a child, sinning had to do with lying or talking in school — things I regularly confessed in those days — and not much else. The church, of course, regarded divorce as sinful then and still does, but I had not been married in the church. So, was I a sinner or not? And did I intend to put myself on the line by asking?

Outside the Paulist Center in the wind, I walked across the common, crossed Tremont Street to West. The dusty shelves and worn spines of the Brattle Book Shop, one of the oldest used book stores in the country, greeted me the same as always. Before the religion/philosophy section on the second floor, I stood and wept for no reason. Today I have some better understanding of how profoundly moved I was by the priest's welcome and his affirmation. I know the courage it must have taken for me to call for the meeting with Rich Colgan followed by the strain of showing up. But I think I worried just then that my return might be at the expense of the connection with my mother. She had done her best, but when I said aloud that it was she who took me from the practice of my faith, I felt disloyal to her.

# ~ 4 ~

# SHOPPING AROUND

A S A WOMAN unaccustomed to asking permission from anyone, the folly of my consulting male clergy for guidance now occurs to me. Where else was I to go? I think that because the priests I initially met on my return were so engaging I did not question the exclusion of women in the hierarchy as much as I did later. Jim Keenan, Rich Colgan — these and others were not policy makers. They were thoughtful and gracious and responsive. I was grateful.

When Father Colgan suggested that I shop around for churches, I imagined a mall on a Saturday afternoon. I thought of a city highway lined with possibilities. I remember the confidence in his voice when he said, "You'll find what you need."

I told no one about my trip to the Paulist Center the previous day, not even my husband, who generally supported me in all things. A secular Jew, he had no use for religion and was particularly harsh on orthodoxy, I thought. Once when a man and a little boy came to our front door, Bibles in hand, he chased them down the path with a broom. At family seders to mark the beginning of Passover, he sometimes irritated others by talking during the ritual. He never said anything against any specific religion. Like most of us, he thought that whatever others did was their own business, as long as they weren't in his face with it. Nevertheless, I was glad when he left early for work the next morning so I could begin my "shopping" without explanations.

The church just around the corner from our house presented an unimpressive exterior of tan brick. Indeed the rectory appeared more grand, though it, too, would have blended into the other suburban houses were it not for the lifesize statue of the Virgin Mary in front. I had once written a short story about the disappearance of just such a statue from just such a rectory, which kept turning up in odd places — the Presbyterian church across town, for example. Passing it on my way to Mass that morning, I was tempted to pat the statue on the head. There was something about the representation of a sacred being spending the winter months outdoors all alone that had never seemed right to me, even if it was only an object made of plaster.

I was thinking about this when I entered the church from the side door at five of nine and heard the voices praying in unison. Was I late? The door brought me to the front of the church. Three pews of old women on their knees saying the rosary lifted their heads and regarded the intrusion though their lips did not stop. "Hail, Mary, full of grace," they intoned. I hurried to a pew behind them, and the priest entered.

"Good morning," he said, much like my old camp director before flag raising each day.

"Good morning, Father," the women answered in unison. The Mass began. "In the name of the Father and of the Son and of the Holy Spirit, Amen." I was able to make the sign of the cross. So gently, so repetitiously had Sister Perpetua taught us first graders the correct sequence that by the time we got to the Holy Ghost — today the Holy Spirit — we moved our left shoulders forward for "holy" and our right for "ghost" in a kind of extracurricular motion that gave us a great kick. Sister didn't seem to mind. After all, a child could only stand there so long beside her desk practicing what she already knew before she made a game of it. We competed to see who could do it faster before Sister insisted on our patience for the other children who got right and left mixed up.

The priest had just finished the "Lord have mercy. Christ have mercy." I was stuck in the English-Latin adjustment. *Kyrie eleison. Christe eleison.* For me in this context, English was the foreign language, and I translated to Latin as if it were the compass that would lead me through the Mass.

Then we were on our feet. "Let us stand now and profess our faith," said the priest.

Oh boy, I thought. I can do this. The Apostles' Creed. "I believe in one God, the Father Almighty, Creator of heaven and earth." That overconfidence was the beginning of my dislocation. Apparently the creed was now a longer prayer with different words — the Nicene Creed, I would later learn. There was even a part of it quite beautiful: "God from God, light from light, true God from true God." But I had no clue what it was supposed to mean. And there was little time to reflect on it as the priest raced through the liturgy. This much was familiar: the speedy saying of the weekday Mass. I would not take communion.

We recited the Lord's Prayer, the Our Father. Except for something about "kingdom and glory" at the end, it was unchanged, though the women raised their arms by their sides, palms open exactly like the statue outside. I considered the action and other additions to the Mass. Did they bring one closer to God, to Jesus Christ? Did it mean that earlier generations missed something important? In these moments, the connection with Jim Keenan's sense of an evolving church or to my father's notions of inconsequential detail was lost.

And now the Sign of Peace. The women hugged one another and came back to shake hands with me. Okay. It wouldn't kill me to touch the hands of strangers, these hands that had prayers on them.

There were no Hail Marys at the end of the service.

"I'm due at the old people's home," the priest said, "where I'm going to play Santa Claus." He patted his rounded belly.

Laughter.

"My schedule is so full I don't know how I'll get everything done," he said. "And I had a toothache yesterday."

"Oooh," said the ladies.

"Not to worry. I'm fine." He all but had his vestments off before leaving the sacristy. "Have a good day, everyone," he said.

"You, too, Father," they answered.

"Dominus vobiscum," I said. Did the Vatican Council really think that the shift from Latin to the vernacular mattered when it remained so rigid on sex? The flat vowels — "The Lord be with you" — thudded on my ears like mud on mud. Why couldn't I just give it up? Jesus, of course, spoke Aramaic, not Latin. I genuflected, crossed myself with holy water, and entered a day full of bright winter sun.

THE SAINT FRANCIS BOOK STORE was on a busy street not far away. I intended to buy a missal for the new liturgy, a guidebook.

"Just wandering," I said to the person in charge, a thin man with a fringe of white hair on the back of his head.

It was a small one-room shop with some few rows of goods and books. "Hark! the Herald Angels Sing" played in the background. Someone I couldn't see was looking, she said, for a gift for a bedridden uncle.

"Listen," said the man with the hair in a stage whisper as if the store were itself a holy place, "here's the perfect thing. Look."

I imagined a woman wrenlike, peering over bifocals, as he held something or pointed to it on a shelf.

"The eyes of the Blessed Mother follow you from every position," he said. "I've got one on my dresser at home. I swear it keeps me pure. It does."

---

*"Just wandering," I said to the person in charge.*

---

The sale was made. The customer, a hefty woman with no glasses, left.

I ambled casually down the aisle to see the perfect thing, the perfect gift, the gift that keeps a person pure. Two feet high — well, maybe sixteen inches — a plastic statue of the Virgin Mary stood, reminiscent of a Disney character, the Seventh Dwarf, or even Santa Claus. And it was true: the eyes followed you everywhere. Silly and sad at once, I hoped I would be able to say nothing, to make no wisecrack. I imagined telling a funny tale about the object at the dinner table. And then I paused. I did not want to be a silly person in a story about a plastic statue with eyes that watched everything. I wanted to come home to my own faith.

After the Florida Mass, the one I talked about to Father Colgan, I had hung around for a bit outside in the hall drinking coffee and getting pieces of donut caught in my throat. I had introduced myself to a few people and explained that I was visiting, but I was unable to sustain a conversation. Adjacent to the hallway was a gift shop with plastic statues and rosaries, holy cards and household fonts. You could buy holy water in small bottles for two dollars.

Now in the little shop on the highway close to home, I chose a child's paper missal and a book by radical nun Joan Chittister. I asked about a rosary of wooden beads. It was at this very point that I remembered that for all these years I had prayed some little bit every day — if only to still a timid heart when it felt threatened, or before sleep after examining my conscience. My conscience? My, my. How far away had I really gone?

That night, I told my husband about the Paulist Center, the Mass, the shop with the statue's roving eyes.

"Good for you," he said. "Tell me everything." He was not surprised. Twice a week since September, he had listened to my summaries of events in the course on moral theology. He had witnessed my excitement about the assigned reading. "When do you go again?"

# ~ 5 ~

# GOOD AND EVIL

I DID GO AGAIN. I tried out most of the local churches.
Nearing the end of the semester at the seminary, I had
been to a dozen different liturgies in as many churches. The
sequence of the Mass became more or less familiar, though it
was commonly subject to alteration. I participated in the celebration of the Eucharist and even occasionally drank the wine
that was now offered in the majority of churches. Catholics,
I discovered, were not enthusiastic singers. This did nothing,
however, to dilute my own enjoyment. Music often carried an
otherwise lackluster liturgy. Choir and strings and even horns
supplemented organ and piano at several churches. Still, I was
brought up short by homilies claiming that only Christians
would have eternal life. And the differences between "praying
for all new mothers" and the "elimination of abortion from the
face of the earth" declared war on moderation. I told myself
that the shift from a medieval institution to a modern forum
had been bound to generate turmoil, but I continued to find
the church experience unsettling. Stained glass may have been
removed to let light in, but this light did not seem to pene-
trate matters of substance. I was unable to find a Mass I could
tolerate. Maybe I expected too much. I hated my need and
my awkwardness, the hope at each service and, more times
than not, the disappointment. I wondered if what I had begun

to call my "fieldwork" in Catholicism had not tarnished my renewal.

Yet an easy camaraderie at the seminary continued alongside its purposefulness without the excessive piety or righteousness I found at liturgies. Clearly I was more comfortable with theory than with practice. I had, after all, spent much of my life in academia. Still, the hospitality I found at the seminary held me in ways that secular institutions had not. With students or staff, at the library or in the ladies' room, it made no difference that I audited only a single course. The sense that we were all in this world together prevailed in a way absent from liturgical experience.

Sometimes when I arrived early for class, I went to the chapel to sit quietly alone. One afternoon, I found a dozen young men and women there on the altar steps. Some few others were in chairs. A man in a yellow sweater spoke softly to the group, and I had to strain to hear each word.

"Who knows what you should do if you find a dollar on the sidewalk?" he said.

Silence.

"Would you pick it up and go buy yourself some ice cream?" he tried again.

"No," said the group in unison, not unlike the women at my first neighborhood Mass.

"That's right," said the young man. "So what would you do?"

Several raised their hands enthusiastically.

"I'd give it to my mother," said one.

"I'd give it to a policeman," said another.

The rows of wooden chairs with short ladder backs reminded me of those at Notre Dame in Paris. I considered the numbers of churches I had visited all over the world during the years that I had seldom entered one in my own country. I remembered the Buddhist temples and monasteries and prayer rooms with their butter lamps where I had been so reverential. I thought about the churches in Bolivia and the Cathedral of San Francisco where the Quaker mother had railed against Catholicism. Because of fire restrictions, it was no longer possible to light candles in most churches anymore the way I had that day in La Paz. Even at the Dalai Lama's temple in northern India altar lamps were electric.

Now at the seminary chapel, a young woman replaced the man who had been asking the questions. "And what would you do if you found money in the street?" she said.

I closed my eyes. Apparently this was a preaching practicum for children, not, as I had assumed, a group of retarded adults on an outing. You had to pay attention or risk collecting the wrong ideas, didn't you? You could be in a hurry and only half-listen or be too quick to judge.

I was glad later to immerse myself in the moral theology lecture. This field work, this investigation, this shopping around business yielded so little beyond a ragged initiation into the current church. On the other hand, reading and discussion were really energizing. Our text and the substantive course packet laid the groundwork for my most compelling questions about the difference between the ethics of being and the ethics of doing.

The being piece concerned the good person, while the doing focused on right actions. Probably the missionaries in Bolivia were okay in their beings — that is, they knew the qualities of being "good." Doesn't everyone? But what about action? What if good people do wrong actions and think they're good? And who decides what's right or wrong? Differing views created the fire in this course. Some students asked, "What would Jesus do?" I considered this clever at first, but after a while it began to seem weaselly to me, some avoidance of putting oneself into the equation as a variable.

Midway through the course, Jim Keenan had introduced the issue of sin — "the overwhelming human capacity for evil" — ameliorated somewhat by redemption. Like a supersalesman, he had spent weeks softening us up with lectures about the love command, by outlining the history of Catholic moral thought, only to zap us with his real message about humans as terrible sinners. He continued the theme, adding one layer after another during the rest of the course.

I wasn't certain what I thought about sin. Our instructor never demanded that others think as he did, which was one reason his arguments drew such close attention. The concept of real evil was not easy to grasp. I had always taken issue, even as a youngster, with the prayer to Saint Michael the Archangel, still regularly said in some churches today at the end of the liturgy:

> Saint Michael the Archangel, defend us in battle. Be our safe-guard against the wickedness and snares of the devil. May God rebuke him, we humbly pray, and do thou, O prince of the heavenly host, by the power of God, cast into hell Satan and all the other evil spirits, who prowl through the world, seeking the ruin of souls.

For one thing, the word "wicked" came to me by means of fairy tales before I heard it in the convent applied to real people. Today as Keenan lectured, I thought I believed that no one was totally evil. I didn't think evil spirits prowled throughout the world. But I knew there were shades of gray here, nuances I missed. I tried, sometimes without success, to avoid situations where I had to judge others. It was so easy to be wrong.

"Give up narcissism," Father Keenan was saying, "and follow Christ."

Matthew McShane, next to me, loved this lecture. "Finally," he smiled, "we've gotten to the heart of the matter."

I took his meaning to be the fact of sin, the prevalence of evil, perhaps even the prowling of Satan throughout the world. The ideas seemed too extreme, too dramatic. Certain other distinctions — intention, follow through, remorse, recompense — needed to be addressed, in my view.

"Real sin and wickedness result from not bothering to love," said Jim.

Now there was something I could get my arms around. Not bothering to love. Not seeing. Not caring. Making another invisible. It was the thing that made me most angry. We have an obligation, I thought, to see, to pay attention to others. Of course, when I thought the group I had just seen in the chapel was handicapped, I looked the other way. I went to Paris and thought about chairs in Notre Dame. I went to Bolivia, to the Himalaya, to India. So much for my obligation to see, to make people visible. It was a small drama but telling. Keenan had spoken about sinning from strength rather than weakness.

"We are deluded into thinking we have self-knowledge, therefore trivializing sin," he said.

How, I wondered, did a person take the time to acquire self-knowledge without being narcissistic?

"It is the privilege of ministry to listen to narratives of struggle. We discover our sins in the act of confession, which illuminates and therefore enables us to acknowledge guilt. We do not have access to sinfulness without confession."

These were difficult and slightly circular concepts, I thought. So much depended on the listener and his or her state of mind.

"The task is to strive to tolerate the ambiguity of how wonderful and how sinful we are," he continued.

If Matthew McShane embraced sinfulness, I embraced ambiguity. Only a math problem could be absolutely right or wrong, I often thought, and even that was too pat.

---

*We have an obligation, I thought, to see, to pay attention to others.*

---

The focus of the early Catholics had been on how to avoid evil. Manuals of all the sins had been given to confessors, similar to books for medical diagnosis. Since Vatican II, the task to be good related to movement toward virtue and secondarily to the avoidance of sinning. I was interested that this thinking paralleled new theories in mental health about focusing more on healthy behavior than on pathology.

Most of us had already read *Letter from a Birmingham Jail* by Martin Luther King Jr. The Christian image of who sits at the table and who does not was still relevant for our time. But equally important to consider was what a person of conviction must be willing to do in order to facilitate inclusiveness, to combat evil. More was required than issuing an invitation. Otherwise, we were merely those "good people who do nothing."

None of us wanted merely to be good.

"Mercy and compassion are the willingness to enter another's chaos," Keenan was saying in his effort to explain at least one path toward virtue. He spoke about the incarnation as just that quality of God's mercy.

As the course wound down, students labored over their required papers and studied in groups for the final exam, an oral. I met with Father Keenan in his office. I'm not sure if I even said that I was trying to return to Catholicism, a fact that was never as big a deal to anyone else as it was to me. It seemed important to thank him for the class and to acknowledge his giftedness. I related the concerns abroad that had led me to his course in moral theology. He suggested some references and offered several of his own experiences he thought might be parallel. We spoke about writing.

But in the end, it was the assumption at the seminary, the fervent belief that each of us has the capability to know God, that reignited my faith. I'm not sure if anyone said this or taught it, but I witnessed before me the struggle of others to understand and to know what they must do. And I took heart.

# ~ 6 ~

# FLORIDA APPARITIONS

W HEN I GOT OFF THE PLANE IN TAMPA a week before
Christmas, the air pressed its weight and humidity and
oppression over me. I had been here maybe a hundred times,
probably more. During the past few years as my mother aged, I
had visited her once each month. The palm trees, the blue skies,
the herons and pelicans, the lovely jacaranda and oleander —
all of these could fool you into imagining a good life here —
golf and tennis and fishing; no winter clothes or blizzards. It
was easy to forget that the land floated only a few feet above
sea level, and that the afternoon rain could pummel the earth
with such force that sometimes you thought everything would
dissolve into its most basic form. You could find an alligator in
your toilet or lizards on your walls. You got a stiff neck from
the air conditioning, and when you visited someone who chain
smoked and kept the heat at eighty-two degrees you wondered
how you'd get through it.

During the flight, I had examined the stack of books I'd
brought about returning Catholics and been disappointed by
the degree of their piety. The "fallen aways" confessed the
sins of their lives apart, admitted there was no satisfactory
life away from Jesus Christ, and, most of all, repented. They
appeared to cower before the rediscovered God even as they
basked in his reflected glory. What about the love command?

What about unconditional forgiveness? One book defended the church's rigid doctrinal positions by referring to the anti-Catholicism of America's earliest days. Priests were tarred and feathered. Crosses were burned in front of Catholic homes. Since many immigrants were unschooled and illiterate, priests decided what the faithful should know and in what depth. I appreciated the context, but the admission that the church had hung on too long to the old ways did not speak to me in this present time.

At the retirement complex where my mother lived now, in her living room crowded with the furniture from another life, I told her that I had decided to return to Catholicism.

"It doesn't surprise me," she said.

And that was it. She rattled the ice cubes in her empty water glass and moved on to another subject — to old age, to the deaths of her friends and husbands, or to the paucity of good bridge games. She planned a swim in the heated pool. Had I brought my bathing suit? Had I gained weight? And so on. She repeated these same things again and again, and I surrendered to the hours and days with her as if her voice itself were a mantra and I were in another place. She rarely had visitors and hardly ever participated in the activities available to her. Even the bridge games were less frequent. Though I met others in the dining room where she ate her dinner who were content, hers was a lonely life. She had kicked and raged into the losses of old age, giving up her house, her car, her possessions, even her hearing. After several falls, she had agreed to use a walker but did so only occasionally. Though she was a difficult woman, her sense of humor remained as keen as her exacting criticism. She was perfectionistic and judgmental, but I had learned to accept her bitterness. She had loved me as she could.

"It's wonderful when our hips touch," she said, the afternoon we plunked ourselves down side by side on the divan in order to leaf through her photograph albums. "It's the only touching I have anymore, you know."

The cigarette smoke swirled around her head, around my head. My eyes burned. I had already opened the door for fresh air, the fresh humid Florida air. My mother was ninety years old. If she wanted to smoke in her own rooms, she had every right to do so. These visits always included reviewing old snapshots. We looked at travel pictures. We examined photos of her friends and family before she was married, when she played tennis, went horseback riding, and belonged to a literary club. She recounted stories about success and happiness that reminded her of a life fully lived. These reminiscences had begun during my childhood when she would carry her albums from the attic to the living room of our house, and I never tired of hearing them. This time was different. She whipped past the family photos of her three sisters together in ribbons and pigtails, my favorites, past the school pictures, beyond those of her athletic achievements, ahead through photos of marriage, the birth of my older sister, to a picture of the home she cherished in a Chicago suburb.

"Tom was always changing jobs," she said, as if it had been my father's major defect. "How I'd worked on those draperies before he came home and told me we were moving to Philadelphia," she said wistfully. We both knew she regarded my father's biggest flaws as illness and death, leaving her alone with two children. She paused at a page now, kept her index finger on the black and white photograph, and took a deep breath. Her cigarette burned itself out in the ashtray, leaving a thin trail of smoke.

"I was pregnant a few years before you were born," she said, uncharacteristically placing me in the story, taking my hand and making a fist around it.

I filled in. "A miscarriage."

"No," she said, "an abortion." The *bore* part was louder than the rest of the word.

"Oh," I said, without missing a beat. The scent of the ashes, the temperature of the room, the black pages of the albums had lulled me into familiarity. I examined the corners that held the photos in place. I read the captions in the white ink my mother had used to identify the hallmarks of her life.

---

*Did she forgive the twenty-seven-year-old, the "wicked woman," by telling her secret aloud? I hoped that she did.*

---

She must have rehearsed this tale often in her mind, because it came out fully formed. "It was still depression times, you know, and we had no money for another baby."

"How . . . " I said.

"I took the trolley down to the old Roosevelt Hotel and had the abortion there." She lit another cigarette.

I imagined a dingy hotel with dark hallways. I blinked. "How much?" I said.

"Twenty-five dollars. I had to borrow the money from a girlfriend. And I was really sick afterward."

Two versions of the story followed. One was that she was home alone with a high fever; in the other, she claimed hospitalization. Perhaps both were true. Neither of us was terribly interested in that part just now. What mattered was this: In

1936, my mother went to a sleazy hotel for an abortion without ever mentioning the experience to my devoutly Catholic
father.

"If only I had been able to be public about it," she said.
"Even now it is not too late to be public."

Eventually, of course, the puzzle of my own birth would
present some questions, but in those first moments, I thought
only of a young woman alone, facing an uncertain invasion
without safety.

"Do you think less of me?" she said.

What was she asking for? I had not lived in that house then,
the house to which she returned from the Roosevelt Hotel.
She herself, the person she later became, no longer lived there;
but the teller of her story, the young woman she was then, sat
next to me, and I rocked her in my arms. I tried to imagine
her walking down the dimly lit hallway of a seedy hotel. Her
husband had quit his job without having another. Along the
streets of the city, people queued up for food. Some sold apples
on corners. Some slept under bridges.

When she continued, she said that my father found out
about the abortion and left her, taking my sister with him. "He
called me a wicked woman," she said. "I never forgave him."

Did I think less of her? Less? More? Why had she made me
the judge?

"Think what it would mean for a ninety-year-old woman
to stand on a soap box and tell the story of the Roosevelt
Hotel," she said, returning to the present. Did she forgive
the twenty-seven-year-old, the "wicked woman," by telling her
secret aloud? I hoped that she did.

I was suddenly exhausted. My bones ached. From the smoke
my eyelids had tiny pins attached to them instead of lashes. A

powerful thirst came over me, and I thought of desert people and camels and bright light. Abortion was never the easy way out. It was a complex decision full of pain and unhappiness. No one I knew who had gone through a procedure to end a pregnancy described the experience as happy or right. But the Catholic concern about unborn children to the exclusion of already living human beings lacked proportion and focus, I thought. It fostered extremists who carried posters of fetuses and prevented thoughtful dialogue. When the abortion issue was paraded out so righteously at liturgies, I had sometimes come close to leaving. Now the pain of my mother's experience entered me as if I breathed iron.

EARLY THE NEXT DAY, a Sunday, I walked along the inland waterway that passed my mother's building when a flock of egrets, nearly a dozen, swung low over the ground, so close the orange of their feet and slender beaks against the white feathers forced me to blink. They called softly, almost but not quite honking.

The church I went to that morning was so packed that I barely got a seat. It was unusual for such an early Mass. The couple next to me introduced themselves and smiled. The music started. Everyone rose. The pews shook like the stands at a football game as the congregation sang "The Banner over Me Is Love" as a gospel tune with arms raised toward the ceiling and hips and shoulders swaying. The priest, a small man with white hair, bounced up the aisle. On one side, the smiling couple nudged me, and, on the other, a young mother holding an infant leaned back and forth against my shoulder to the beat of the music. Against the front wall, a projector displayed the lyrics. We clapped and danced in our places. It was wonderful and horrible at once. This was a Catholic church? A terrific kids' choir saved the day as the celebrant went through the motions of the liturgy and homily. I had five more days before going home.

And then we were all standing again. Following the lead of the choir, the congregation began a slow chant, almost whispering, "Come, Jesus, come." We clapped softly, slowly, building a rhythm, as the chanting got ever louder. "Come, Jesus, come. Come, Jesus, come." The moment of consecration was attenuated, until the shouting became a roar. "COME, JESUS, COME." The priest lifted his hands with the host. A collective sigh filled the church. It was all too much. Though I was in the middle of a pew, I stumbled across the others. The blatant sexuality of the act was appalling.

In the vestibule, two women tending a small group of toddlers talked quietly by a door.

"Are you all right?" one said.

"I can't believe it," I said.

"Oh, I know," said the other. "It's awful, isn't it?" She was a heavy woman whose face was round and beautiful as the sun.

"I love it," said the first one. "Brings a little pep to the church."

"You're crazy," said the other woman. "Crazy. Pay no attention to her."

Smiling, they elbowed each other and touched the heads of the children around them.

Just before I'd left for Florida, a priest claiming to minister to returnees on-line responded to my inquiry by saying, "I'll bet Jesus is glad you're back." I had found the remark infantilizing and trivial, however well-intentioned. For some reason, I thought of it now. I thought about the Paulist Center and

the seminary. I remembered the delicate calls of the snowy
egrets that morning. My dislocation from the Catholicism I
once knew was profound.

SOME YEARS BEFORE THIS PRESENT TRIP, the image of a
madonna on a large plate of glass in a local finance building
covered the front pages of all the Florida papers. I read that
thousands of believers made their way there every day to worship. They came from out of town, from across the country,
and around the globe. I went there late one afternoon. The
image, at the intersection of two busy highways, was visible
from the road. Its striking colors — the purple and yellow and
blue-green of a prism — rose for three stories. Women, men,
and children ran toward the periphery of the building in a car-
nival spirit, stopped, before slowly walking forward with their
flowers and candles and messages. A policeman told me that
people arrived and left at the rate of six hundred an hour.

"What do you think about this?" I asked him.

"I just want to keep everybody safe, ma'am," he told me.

That did not appear to be difficult. Most simply knelt on
the macadam in complete silence. Others carried placards with
messages. One said, "Free my father from jail." Above the
building a three-quarter moon began its rise next to a bill-
board that said "Tarpon Springs Casino Cruises Sails Twice
Daily." Inside an adjacent gas station, there were commemora-
tive mugs and T-shirts for sale. By coincidence an international
convention of glass scientists was in town. They could find no
explanation for the image of the madonna.

I had not knelt before the plate glass window that day. I had
remained on the edge of the parking lot where I listened to
the low murmurs of individual prayers, the scraping of feet as

people moved forward and back, waiting their turns and then leaving. The day after my mother told me about her abortion, as I drove away from the church that so desperately urged Jesus to come to them, I remembered that I had stood before the madonna image as an outsider, and that the believers' longing for grace had been palpable.

DURING THE REMAINDER OF MY VISIT, my mother repeated the abortion story, editing one rendition after the other. Determined to get it right, she added details: the several trolleys to the hotel, a high fever, a second hospital stay, a woman in a bloody gown performing the procedure on a wooden table in the hotel room, the separation from my father.

Did my father tell his folks about the abortion?

She never asked him. He came back. They never spoke of it.

Didn't she understand what marrying a Catholic would mean?

Her family had no religion. How could she have possibly known? She knew nothing about kneeling to say the rosary after dinner or fasting on holy days. She had never imagined that civilized people would choose not to use birth control. She agreed to be baptized. She agreed to raise her children Catholic. Wasn't that enough?

THIS WAS ONLY THE BEGINNING of my mother's confessions to me about the things in her life she regretted, though the abortion seemed her most troubling secret. My return to the church appeared to open some door for her to clear her conscience, as if I myself had been anointed her confessor. She went on for many months about how Catholicism had ruined her marriage to my father before she was able to remember again that she had once loved him.

Eventually, I reflected on what these painful revelations meant in terms of my own place in the family. I had often wished I had known my father better. But did I want to know the man who called my mother a wicked woman? The man who left her all alone when she was so sick? I wondered but did not ask if the price for my father's return was another child. But I understood why he and I were so close, and why I had never seen his family again after he died.

When a parent lives into old age, you get the chance to say everything, to let go, to ask questions. I forgave my mother for separating me from the Catholic side of the family and from my faith. As she talked and talked, on and on, smoking one cigarette after another, the sunlight in the room where we spent so many hours touched the gigantic crystal ashtray that was always full. Sometimes the rays glimmered like prisms, reminding me of the madonna in the finance building windows. The purple and yellow and green entered my mother's living room as miracles of color and then disappeared. Though I never returned to the apparition, I heard that several million people had been there to worship.

*Part II*

# FAITH

# ~ 7 ~

# PRIORY

"AT THE RISK OF PUSHING THE ENVELOPE, I'd say you have a lot in common with Jesus."

*Pushing the envelope. A lot in common with Jesus.* These were not the words spoken at my first meeting with Father John Allard, but they came close to characterizing our association over the next year.

It was late February when I navigated the icy, elegant drive into the seventy-five acre estate that was Saint Stephen's Priory on my way to meet the Dominican priest. Snowy trees, tall and straight as sentinels, guarded the property in silence. True or not, I had the idea that freezing temperatures purified the air, and I breathed deeply, feeling very healthy indeed. A few souls braved the chill, walking the grounds this late afternoon. Mercifully, the extremes of weather had called me to slow my pace after the holidays.

Jim Keenan's lectures had resumed, dynamic as ever, but the new course, Virtue Ethics, was more directly related to specific issues in ministry than the previous one in moral theology. The questions raised at the outset — Who am I? Who shall I become? How shall I get there? — clearly applied to all, yet I found only the third one provocative. The excitement about auditing classes at the seminary had waned as I came to grips with the fact that it was not, after all, designed for refugees like me.

And that is how I had begun to think of myself: as a refugee, a person torn away from her origins with no possibility of return to the same place. Though this was well before the sexual abuse scandal that later rocked the church to its roots, it was even then an institution devastated by controversy in its reforms. I was in the throes of learning that my faith was whole but that the church itself — the human church — was fractured. My associations at the seminary gave me some of what I required. But I had begun to know that I needed something else. New thoughts, or old ones newly reflected, had grown too large to hold on my own.

I stamped the snow from my boots outside the priory's fieldstone home and stepped inside. The hall and two living rooms where I waited with their elegant dark wood reminded me of the motherhouse of the Sisters of Mercy, which had also been a turn-of-the-century estate acquired by the church. Saint Stephen's, run by the Dominican friars, served primarily as a retreat and renewal center for priests and nuns, though programs for the laity had been initiated in recent years. The rich scarlet tones of the oriental carpets brought to mind the eternal flame, no longer present in sanctuaries, that once indicated the presence of the Eucharist. I had no notion of why it had been removed. In the corner of the hall, a grandfather clock chimed the hour. To its right a bulletin board held half a dozen scraps of paper on which one-sentence petitions for prayer were written.

A young man entered from a side hallway and the two of us shook hands. Dominican, Paulist, Jesuit — the nuances that marked the differences among the orders of priests were unclear. To me, a priest was a priest was a priest. One of my classmates at the seminary worked at the priory and had suggested I meet with Father Allard. Up close, I saw that he was older than he appeared at first. Perhaps he was forty. We were about the same height. He had the fair complexion and blue eyes of those with red hair and the surefootedness of a runner. He wore glasses. In those first moments of our meeting I saw a man at once comfortable with himself and vulnerable. From the priory's website I had learned that he had been a missionary in the mountains of South Africa, that he had a Ph.D. from Catholic University. He led me to a wing of the building, down a narrow hallway to a newer section with small rooms and offices.

"I need help," I said, as we settled ourselves in one of them. Did I need help? Or was I still seeking information? "I'm not sure," I added.

"Maybe you'd prefer a woman." He had said this to me on the telephone, and he repeated it now as we faced one another.

A woman? Would I prefer to speak with a woman? I didn't know. I didn't think so. I needed to know the state of the current tradition, I thought, before speaking with women about the church. What did it mean to be Catholic today? What about the sacraments and the rules and actual worship? Could a nun talk about these things with authority? I had the idea that women religious might be either too pious or too radical. I wanted to find a place in the church without that kind of pressure. Eventually I would have to address the issues that made church women so polarized. I knew that, but I would not do it just yet.

John Allard had grown up in Rhode Island, he told me, and majored in French at Middlebury College. He taught in the Midwest before being ordained. After returning from Africa, he served as chaplain at Memorial Sloan-Kettering, the famous cancer institute in New York. His father had died of cancer. I remember thinking that these personal revelations did not seem burdensome, but that they served as points of information. He was the director of the sabbatical program at the priory for nuns who came from around the world for rest and renewal.

I spoke about Bolivia and my travels in the Himalaya. I told him about the Buddhist monastery built into the side of a mountain in Bhutan where I had felt God's presence so acutely. I had studied Buddhism, I said, and been at home with its rituals, but I had not embraced it as my own the way so many other westerners had. The lama at the monastery had given me his room for my use, and at night as I lay in the stillness, the low murmurs of voices outside held me in a safety I was unable to understand, even as I told the tale to John Allard. But I think now that the stillness and reverence must have mirrored my early life in the convent school and stirred something in me. As children, we were rarely permitted to speak — not at meals or between classes or at night. Most of us pushed against it, tested it, though we ultimately gave in to the silence. It encouraged us, I think, to live within our beings and to avoid distraction. Ultimately, what had most attracted me to Buddhist culture was its similarity with my own faith and experience.

John Allard spoke about his work in South Africa and asked me why I thought I was so interested in mountain people. He said what he could offer me in terms of his other time commitments. He came across as a man totally without guile.

I found myself trying to convince him that we could work together. I didn't need a writer, I told him. I needed an association with someone whose experience could give me perspective on my own interaction with the church. I decried the present

liturgy and my awkwardness with it. Such complaints probably came out as angry whining. I knew so little then about
the general disgruntlement with the Mass.

"Our liturgy here isn't too bad," he said. "Eleven on Sundays." He said this as an announcement rather than with any
urging to it.

I liked that. But the prospect of trying out another Mass
made me sigh. "It's like a series of blind dates," I said, not
thinking, "this search for the right fit." I'd read somewhere that
the head of the Boston archdiocese, Cardinal Bernard Law, had
mandated that Catholics attend Mass at their local parishes,
that he was against "supermarket" Catholicism.

"So," said Father Allard, as we rose to leave the office,
"you're talking about a tutorial."

In the Himalaya, Buddhist monks had frequently asked me
with whom I studied in America. I had never had a tutor. But
yes, that was exactly what I wanted.

After our meeting, the two of us walked to the priory library,
a small room at a lower level. I was free to check out books
here, he said. We walked among the stacks and he identified
each section as if he were a guide and I a stranger in an exotic
land. He would give some thought, he said, to what books
might be useful for me.

I was quite overwhelmed by his kindness. I *was* in an exotic land. Once when I suffered from acute altitude sickness in
Nepal, a Tibetan woman had taken me to her home and fed
me thick yak butter tea. She had rested my head in her apron
and rubbed turquoise stones over my head and neck and arms.
John Allard was also a stranger to me that day, and though I
was hardly sick, I had been spiritually vacant for such a long
time that I received his hospitality as an elixir.

"A prudent person has both feet on the ground. The prudent person must be attentive to detail, anticipate difficulties and measure rightly. The first sign of real prudence is finding the right person to give advice." So Jim Keenan was saying then in his Virtue Ethics course.

Prudence was hardly at the top of my list of virtues. I had often acted impulsively, taking serious matters lightly and making too much out of the trivial. Was John Allard the right person to give me advice? I didn't think I needed advice. I needed the means to connection.

A navy sky ascended through the rows of trees as I drove away from the priory. I thought I heard crows but saw only shadows. The clear air promised a starry evening.

THE FOLLOWING SUNDAY I attended Mass in the priory chapel. Three rows of choir pews faced each other in the simple room that was more like a Quaker meeting house than the Gothic buildings of my childhood. Behind the altar, a modern palladium window overlooked woods and the Charles River. A rose-colored carpet covered the floor. John Allard sat at the organ.

"Did Jesus die?" whispered a child behind me, halfway through the liturgy.

I strained for the parent's response.

"Who killed him?" said the child.

The usual worries about misstepping plagued me throughout this Mass made intimate by its small congregation. Like a teenager at a party, I assumed all eyes were on me. I laughed at my foolishness but nonetheless watched carefully to see how people lined up for communion. By the final blessing, I knew this was a special place, that it could even be *my* place. Thirty or forty sisters on sabbatical lined the sacristy. When we recited The Lord's Prayer, the couple in front of me wove their arms around each other's backs. John Allard's musical direction was lively, and the organ had a fine sound. There was no prayer about Satan prowling the world. A basket on a pedestal for voluntary collections in the hallway replaced the Offertory. The sermon, a homily on intimacy, had depth and synthesis. The prior spoke about "the call to be by letting go." Later I would learn that he had given up the law for the priesthood. Self-effacing and sincere, yet full of humor and respect, he knew he preached to the converted. We existed for him as children of God more than as sinners. Afterward there was coffee and conversation in the adjacent living rooms. It was an eminently civilized experience. There was no prayer for the unborn.

---

*Like a teenager at a party, I assumed all eyes were on me.*

---

The Mass marked the first time I heard the consecration blessing: "We have this bread to offer, fruit of the earth and made by human hands . . . " and later of the wine, "We have this wine to offer, fruit of the vine and made by human hands. . . . " The prayer made me believe that some traces of poetry existed in the modern Mass. Unhappily, the prior would be reassigned not long after I found him, but not before I understood that the liturgy could be both sacred and relevant after all.

DURING MY SECOND MEETING with John Allard, we spoke about forgiveness. I was so embarrassed not to know what I was doing, I said. What if people knew I was an impostor? I told the story about Matthew McShane. "Are you a Catholic or what?"

"Why wouldn't they be glad to welcome you back?" he said. "Have you forgotten about the lost sheep?"

"You mean I could just tell people I've been gone and come back?" As I said this, I knew it was true. It was true and simple and had been there all the time.

But though John Allard was kind and soft-spoken, he was also tough on me. It was one of the things I would come to appreciate most about him — that, like any good teacher, he would nudge me to widen my scope. It was at our second meeting that he made the remark about pushing the envelope and Jesus.

I remember that I admired his courage in challenging me, but that I was totally unprepared and could not respond. My mind spun. I thought of a bird trapped in a garage. The urge to laugh bubbled up, receded, but remained in my throat. Had I gotten myself into a weird situation here? Jesus? I had something in common with Jesus? When I neither slithered off the chair nor fled from the room, I decided to consider the idea. I felt as if I might have been running for a long time. I did not imagine that John Allard meant his remark to deify me in some way, but only to point out that Christ had been the model for my actions, however successful or failed. A small insight glimmered somewhere for me outside that room. Maybe it was then that I began to know that I could not alter my species or color or spiritual roots, even torn from them as I had been.

True to his word, the Dominican brought several books for me to read, and he recommended others as well as passages from scripture. We arranged to meet every few weeks. This would continue throughout the spring and into the following year. Yet it seems to me now that despite his being a Catholic priest, my tutor did not have his own agenda for me. Perhaps that was because I was already such a convinced Catholic, but I think it had more to do with the quality of his respect for all people and their personal truths. He never specifically outlined in what ways we differed — and I never asked — only that he was "probably more conservative."

I did not bring any major crises in my external life to John Allard. Still, the personal and the spiritual could not really be separate compartments. I seemed to be okay with God but I felt less successful in living a Catholic life, whatever that meant. As I attempted to integrate what I felt with what I knew and was learning, I became intense, determined, occasionally obsessive, and always appreciative. I was frequently confused and irritated. It was not until several years after our initial meeting that I remembered the definition of compassion I had learned in the moral theology course at the seminary: *the willingness to enter another's chaos.*

# ~ 8 ~

# ANGER AND FORGIVENESS

WOMEN ARE SUPPOSED to have a terrible time expressing anger. We are socialized to cry and wring our hands but not to lash out. We are less likely than men to punch someone, to commit a crime, though more apt to attempt suicide. Until recently, women had little access to athletics. Even now, that outlet may still be regarded as not quite feminine.

The sisters in the sabbatical program at the priory come from missions throughout the world for rest and reflection and renewal. They stay at the priory in private rooms and attend seminars and prayer services as they wish. The option for weekly spiritual direction also exists. Theoretically at least, the seminars are open to the public. Halfway through the spring term in March, I signed up for the six-week course on anger and forgiveness. I was the only lay person in the class.

In the months that I had been actively returning to faith, there had been many tender moments of recognition for me. However I railed against the liturgy, the simple act of blessing myself with holy water as I entered and left the church never ceased to feel cleansing. Sometimes after receiving the Eucharist, tears rolled down my cheeks, despite the chewing issues and the distractions of who knelt and who did not. When the instructor began the course that day by explaining that Latin *vulnerare* means to wound, my heart opened once again.

"We are most angry when we are most vulnerable," Father M. said.

It was not a new notion for me. Most of us cannot tolerate exposure for too long and mask it defensively. Yet a weight I had not fully acknowledged — the possibility of woundedness related to my return to the church — settled briefly in my being and then slid away.

I wondered why a priest, even one with a Ph.D. in psychology, should be teaching in a program for women, particularly on a topic with such differences in male-female behavior. His choice of books indicated his own awareness of the issues. Both selections were written by women. I had, however, found them disappointing.

"Too much jargon," I said when he asked our reactions to the reading and no one else spoke up.

Silence.

"Too touchy feely," I added, not knowing when to keep quiet.

More silence.

"But I liked the covers," I said.

"I'm glad of that," said Father M.

The degree of deference by the sisters to the priest astonished me, and I didn't get it right away. We had all been early and had gotten acquainted before class. They were teachers and nurses, hospital administrators and school principals, as well as parish assistants and contemplatives. Some of their orders had closed after Vatican II, and they had joined others. Several still wore abbreviated habits and veils, but most did not. They had loved their experience at Saint Stephen's Priory, they told me. Some hated to leave. Others were anxious to get back to their work. I learned that many were near retirement age or in transition between assignments. By this time in March, nearly at the end of their sabbaticals, they had bonded quite happily, it seemed, though they were quick to include me among them. They were strong, experienced, no-nonsense women. Yet in the seminar they rarely spoke.

Father M. developed his lecture about the anger-forgiveness theme by making good use of the story of the prodigal son. I loved parables for their drama and mystery and openness to interpretation.

---

*"How much anger must a woman hold before acting?" I said.*

---

"Take all the parts," he said. "Imagine the father's joy at seeing his long lost son. Imagine the shame of the son who has been lost and the anger of the son who has stayed at home to do his duty. Each has something to forgive."

I had heard him say Mass several times on Sundays since I had come to the priory. He was a superior liturgist, and his homilies were inspiring. I was not surprised to discover some months later that he was a poet. Shame was the umbrella under which my awkwardness in the liturgy existed. It was the precise word for so much of what I had endured on my return home to the church.

"God causes our hearts never to leave us alone," said Father M. "The struggle with the unforgiving heart doesn't let up." He went on to talk about the rage of the son who had done all the right things by staying at home to please his

father. No doubt the good son wanted to punch out the prodigal. It would be better to endure the feelings. "Sometimes it's
premature to get rid of pain and helplessness."

"It's different for women," I said.

Silence.

"How much anger must a woman hold before acting?" I
said. "I don't think that women need to be encouraged to hold
on to pain and helplessness."

"I'm not saying that one should forget or excuse or endure
smothering conflict," he said. "Keeping waters calm doesn't
save drowning people."

"Wait a minute," said one sister. "I want to write that down,
that business about keeping waters calm."

"Write in capital letters," I said.

"Good idea," said another, a sister from Kentucky who
seemed to draw out the vowels into a full sentence.

I wanted to ask about prodigal daughters but did not. There
was no reason to put too fine a point on my views. The priest
had given me no cause to complain about his teaching, and
I thought that perhaps I had already said too much. I think
that after the seminary reading and that recommended by John
Allard I found the material for this course a bit light and felt
insulted for the nuns. I would quickly discover that it was my
outspokenness that endeared me to them.

Sometimes, they told me, they felt violated by others in their
lives — those with whom they lived or whom they served —
but that they had no means of expression for their feelings
of hurt or anger. A friend might be unkind or a priest too
demanding. Yet seminar participants were reluctant to say
anything negative, especially about priests, to the priest who
taught our seminar.

"Anyone in religious life has occasion to be angry," Father M. was saying one day. Remembering my presence, he looked at me apologetically.

I did not think religious life differed that much from regular living but said nothing. I had spent much of my life in communal groups — from the convent and summer camp to the Quaker school and college dorms.

When he asked for examples and no one spoke, I nudged the sister next to me, a woman in her seventies from Missouri.

She shook her head and whispered, "You go ahead and tell."

"I've heard," I said, "that sometimes sisters who count the hosts for Sunday Mass can over- or undercount."

"And then," another sister, a tiny woman from the Philippines, picked up the thread, "they yell at you."

"Every week," another nun said, "after Mass the same priest phones to complain to me."

"Parish life can be so difficult for priests today," said our instructor. "The men are so alone."

Silence.

Who cared about them? This was not about them. This was about the sisters in this group. It was about being made invisible by another person's sense of entitlement.

"But," I said, "there's no reason why a sister should be abused."

"You're right, of course," the priest said. He was a nice man, a priest who himself was overburdened, I thought, working at a counseling center as well as teaching here.

Silence.

"It's not like you count the hosts wrong on purpose," said a nun from Ireland. "Why don't you say something? I'd certainly say something."

"If he starts at you, you could just hang up," said another.

"She couldn't hang up."

"But what could she say?"

"Sometimes," I said, "you can write a script for yourself."

Laughter.

"You could say," someone said, a hospital comptroller from Baltimore, "that you are doing your best and that his anger isn't going to make you do any better."

The sister in question giggled.

The course had not been designed, I gathered, to teach people how to react to the anger of others in ways that protected them. We could pray for abusers, but there was no acknowledgment of the possibility of taking the power for ourselves. Nor was there discussion about what to do with our own rage. I thought there was an important physical component that gnawed at a person if it went unexpressed. On the other hand, this was not my course to teach. I quite liked Father M., but he seemed to be caught in the same pattern as the sisters. We were all trained to believe that priests were a rung above us in the hierarchy. He was not condescending, but I noticed he spoke to me with some of the same deference the nuns offered him.

It was easier to speak about justice for others than for ourselves. The sisters rarely used the first person when they spoke, either in class or outside informally. When we spoke about Martin Luther King's *Letter from the Birmingham Jail*, there was a sense that we were on safer ground and that whatever our personal issues, they were too small to bring up again.

Jim Keenan often said that it was the western focus on individualism and self-interest that led us away from God. Yet he also exhorted students never to use saints as role models, calling them "maladjusted" or "neurotic." I guessed that asceticism had had its day.

This would have been news to the nuns I met at the renewal center who shared tea bags and took notes on the backs of envelopes and other scraps of paper. I thought how deeply buried their own voices were from themselves and wished each could know something of her unique power. It would be that wish that several months later would lead me to propose a workshop in writing for the sisters in the renewal program.

As the anger and forgiveness seminar progressed, I often remembered the Buddhist nuns I had met abroad who also seemed to live in the shadow of male dominance. In Dharamsala in northern India, the home of the Tibetan refugees, I saw women carrying boulders from the site that would become an addition to their nunnery. I watched them dig the ground, mix cement, and after a long day of manual labor, sit a level below the abbot at prayer.

As I tried to hold my present and past together it often seemed as if one hand grabbed at the wind and the other was caught inside the eye of a growing storm. I thought of the well-appointed rectories where parish priests now lived such lonely lives, according to Father M. How many nuns, I wondered, played golf on their days off? My association with the sisters on renewal brought the inequities between women and men in religious life to the fore. I had been willing to ignore the fact that the Catholic hierarchy — those old men gathered together for Vatican II — was male, that its pronouncements discriminated terribly against women. This would no longer be possible.

I would have to think about what that would mean for me. Could I support a church that refused to allow women to preach? I didn't know. Was it possible that the church still advised women who were abused by their husbands to remain married to them? Did Catholic women who wished to use birth control believe they were sinful? I wondered if retirement funds for nuns equaled those of priests. Probably not.

On a question and answer forum on-line for returning Catholics, a priest had written that those who had been divorced or who were not married in the church were barred from receiving the Eucharist. The statement had had no effect on my own actions. These were man-made rules. Though the marriage issue was not one my father brushed aside in his day, my own conscience was clear on that score. Still, it had been the law that had excluded me and many others for forty years.

This female-male business was more subtle than canon law. It could be insidious. It could take away the right a person had to speak with the authority of her own voice to the meaning of her own experience.

# ~ 9 ~

# ASH WEDNESDAY

T HE ANGER AND FORGIVENESS SEMINAR ought to have provided a perfect segue into Lent. It had always seemed to me that the season permitted, indeed encouraged a person to go to a quiet place inside herself. If we refrained from sweets or were extra kind to our parents and siblings we would be closer to God, the nuns suggested. My intentions had usually peaked on Ash Wednesday. Failure occurred within twenty-four hours. But even as a nonpracticing Catholic, I had marked the day with the knowledge that Lent was a time for reflection. The forty-day journey seemed to me to be the chance to think differently, to consider the ways in which one might wish to be good, both internally and externally, to contemplate the direction or redirection of a life.

My first Ash Wednesday as a returning Catholic, I attended an early Mass in our town center. I had been several times to the old church. The music had been rigorous and the homilies not too pious, but it was an active family parish with lots of kids, noisy kids, so I had stopped going there. That morning I bowed my head with others of the standing room only crowd who received ashes in the ancient ritual of atonement. "Ashes to ashes, dust to dust." I loved the way the church calendar paralleled the growing season. I loved being part of something greater than this moment. As I thought about the day ahead —

how long would I leave the ashes on my forehead? — I was filled with love for this church, my church.

After the Eucharist, before the final blessing, a man in a gray suit and red necktie moved forward. One point of his white shirt collar stuck out at an odd angle. He held the elbow of a young woman whom he led to the pulpit. Still immersed in the ritual of the ashes, I hardly heard his introduction. The woman had brown shoulder-length hair that hung a bit over a pale face. When she began to read from what looked like several pages and color rose to her cheeks and neck, I knew she was not listing Lenten events in the parish. Her shoulders were rounded and seemed to bracket the words as if they were parentheses and she was reluctant to let her message slip through them.

"I lived in sin with alcohol," she said, "until I found Jesus."

I looked around me. No one moved or reacted or left the church.

The woman said her name and continued. The sheets of paper rattled next to the microphone. Was she going to weep?

"God's plan was for me to suffer," she said. "I grew up in a dysfunctional family. This led me to make the wrong choices. I got involved with a man who beat me, the way my father had beaten me, when I was still a teen."

My hands closed into fists beside me on the pew. A testimonial? The woman went on. She went from one man to another, from one year to another. She went on and on and on. She had three children, she said. Each one had his own terrible tale. Lost. She had been lost for a long time until one day Jesus found her. Perhaps she spoke for five or ten minutes. It seemed like thirty.

The priest gave the final blessing. He did not comment on the woman's public confession. I filed out with the others, enraged, my face beating with sweat. It was one thing to hear from priests about their cancer or dental appointments. These had been distractions. But to bring a troubled woman out on Ash Wednesday to remind parishioners of their own sinfulness?

I wish now I had had the guts that day to approach the pulpit and confront those who allowed, who possibly even encouraged, the young woman, the lost woman to speak. Would they have escorted me out like a lunatic or had me arrested? Would it have made any difference?

Outside on the sidewalk, I turned to an elderly couple. "So," I said, "what did you think of the testimonial?"

They looked at one another, then at me, shrugged, and walked away.

I wondered if the young woman was all right. What effect did this self-exposure have on her? And who was the man who had brought her forward? Perhaps she had not only found Jesus, but another abusive partner as well.

I approached a hefty woman of my own age in a pink sweat shirt. "Can I ask you a question?" I said. "Excuse me."

"Sure," she said. "Is something wrong?"

"What did you think about that? About that speech just now?"

She laughed with lovely shining teeth. Her mascara and eye shadow had been applied perfectly. "You never know what's going to happen in there," she said. "You try to immunize yourself." She regarded me, waiting for a response, and when I said nothing, she crossed the street to her car, a long steel gray Cadillac.

The priest stood outside the church shaking hands with his departing flock. I wondered why nothing happened, why no one said anything. What good was it to witness suffering if you did nothing about it? Was I going to speak to the priest? What kind of place was this? Had the Catholic Church become some sort of public confessional? I walked slowly up the stairs to the landing where he was still greeting the congregation. I went back into the church and looked for the man with the gray suit. I looked for the woman herself.

"You should be ashamed of yourself." This is what I would say to her sponsor.

The church was empty now. I regarded the pulpit. You could still smell ashes. It was the same old thing, wasn't it? I witnessed what appeared, to me at least, a wrongful act — the exploitation of pain — and didn't know my obligation. I was no Good Samaritan, no holy person. But the wounded woman had peeled back her skin to show herself. Outside, the priest and another man spoke cheerfully about the end of winter. I turned my back and walked away. I touched my forehead and looked at the blackness on my finger.

Not long before this I had given a talk at the local library about caring for aging parents. People often remained afterward filled with the pain of their dilemmas. They found others like themselves whose elderly parents provided special challenges. Sometimes they stayed to speak with me. They were often tired and scared and isolated in their caregiving.

This woman who thought God's plan for her was suffering — how would she know she had been heard? Or was the humiliation of public confession supposed to be part of her penance? Perhaps others had spoken to her after the Mass, but I did not think so. Her words belonged at an AA meeting, I thought, or in group therapy. But I could have been wrong. The church had changed in so many ways. The woman with the teeth had been right. You never knew what would happen at Mass. I supposed that people learned to listen selectively, or maybe not at all.

I went home, phoned the rectory, and left a voice message. When I did not hear back, I wrote a letter. Not only had the speaker herself been exploited, but so had the congregation. We were a captive audience. We had not been given a choice. But I did not mail the letter. I was in no position to tell others what they should do. The testimonial had rendered me once again a visitor in what had been my church only minutes before during the anointing of the ashes.

Thomas Merton writes about attending, that is, awareness, the value of listening. I think today we would call it "tuning in." I was reading *The Seven Storey Mountain* then at the suggestion of John Allard. The book documents Merton's conversion to Catholicism and his becoming a Trappist monk. How was it possible to attend, to listen to another and then walk away?

What had this woman been asking for? Was it understanding and forgiveness like my mother? My fear was that she asked for nothing, that her message was directed to other sinners — to us — to repent.

When I began the Merton book, I wondered at first if my father and I had read it together as we had done with *Man of Molokai*, the book about Father Damien de Veuster, the priest who lived on a Pacific island among lepers. Both had been among those on his bookshelves. But when I got into it, I realized *The Seven Storey Mountain* was too complex, too interior for a child to have grasped. The wildly popular Merton book was really about privilege making its way to ritual and faith and eventually to silence and retreat. I had been drawn to tales of those without privilege, to the children of Charles

Dickens, to Oliver Twist and David Copperfield, and even to Pim in *Great Expectations.* Yet it was another book on my parents' shelves called *Mother India,* a shocking revelation about children as young as seven being sold off in marriage to much older men, that told me the most about what girls could expect from their lives. And these were the lucky ones. Many infant girls were routinely killed at birth.

> *This woman who thought God's plan for her was suffering — how would she know she had been heard?*

Maybe it was too great a leap backward to compare the woman in the pulpit to the female children in early twentieth-century India. I didn't think so. Reading Merton made me understand my own longing — that of an imperfect human being for God. But I wondered what good faith and longing were if you were helpless to act in the face of suffering.

I asked my classmates in the anger and forgiveness seminar about the testimonial. When one of them called it "unconscionable," I felt the relief of personal validation, though I remained puzzled about why others in the congregation seemed not to share my reactions. I did not ask the sisters if they would have protested the woman's public confession, either at the time or afterward. I felt certain they would not.

John Allard responded to my e-mail describing the Ash Wednesday event, finding it "baffling." I used him as a barometer of what was reasonable in the liturgy and what was unusual, or in fact, bizarre. He did not let me down. "The line about 'God's plan for me to suffer' is troubling," he said.

Nevertheless, I could see that I would have to learn to pick my battles, that I could not continue to react to each perceived injustice. I wished again for my father, for the opportunity to talk about what was consequential and what was not.

THE COMING OF SPRING quelled lengthy days of Boston's dark winters, though the leaves appeared more delicate this year just before opening. A pair of cardinals returned during the second week of Lent. One morning, I went outside for the newspaper and a bird's call punctured the light like a shard of glass. When I looked up, it was silent. Same old bluejay, I thought — with its perfect see-saw pitch. Even the wood-peckers took their places high on the same telephone poles as the previous season. Daffodils in the garden came up golden as the eyes of tigers.

I had not forgotten the testimonial on Ash Wednesday but its sting had vanished. There was too much for me to learn about the new Catholicism to dwell on the missteps of others. Just when the church became familiar, something else would cause me to lose my bearings and upset my tenuous balance with it. They were small things: There was no holy water in the fonts during Lent, for example, and the statues that were once covered with purple cloth had been mostly removed. Statues, like sin and penance and the rosary and stained-glass windows, had gone out of favor. As far as I could note, however, no-body removed the gigantic crucifixes with the replicas of Christ affixed to them. The newer churches generally had crosses with-out bodies, but the older ones retained their graphic depictions of the fragile limbs, the nails, the crown of thorns, even rep-resentations of blood. In the context of Vatican II's focus on redemption rather than suffering, the reminder appeared out of step.

Rain moistened the earth, and new growth appeared. The vulnerability of all creatures to the whims of weather and art made me more alive. Some years before, I had planted English ivy around the base of a locust tree in the center of our yard. Its shiny, heart-shaped leaves now rose fifty feet over the rough bark of the trunk and adjacent branches. One afternoon, I pulled a few dead twigs from a vee in the tree nearly out of my reach. Sticks, grass, and other objects streamed out. Nut shells and string and leaves. Before I could think what it might be, a dreadful screeching froze me in motion. A squirrel bolted across the garden, squawking and chattering, puffed and huge and angry.

I backed away and lifted a rake in defense. "I'm sorry," I said. "I didn't know."

On the limb above me, its mouth moved so rapidly in protest and opened so wide that I imagined a full set of teeth. Its webbed feet were black and powerful and confident.

"Oh, I'm so sorry," I said again. "Really." I regarded the pile of stuff at the foot of the tree. A person could spend hours, even days watching squirrels and birds build their nests, piece by piece, treasure by treasure.

Later that day I saw the animal begin again in another, higher place in the locust tree. And that is what we do — what all of us do, if we can. When we return to our homes and find them destroyed, we start over.

## ~ 10 ~

# PEORIA

THE MAGNIFICENT TWIN SPIRES of Saint Mary's Cathedral rose against a cornflower sky. I ran my fingers over the exquisite Anamosa walls at the entryway. In early April, the white stone still held the central Illinois winter. A plaque honored Father Marquette and the other Jesuits who came to the prairie in the seventeenth century. Inside, the familiar scent and the stained glass issued their ancient invitation. My father had attended this church every day when he went to Spalding Institute, the boys' Catholic high school in the same complex of buildings. My grandparents also worshiped here after they moved into the city from the farm in the early twenties.

This was the first of a three-day visit to Peoria. My cousin Angela sat next to me in the pew. We had only met the one time I had visited her mother many years before this.

"I'm not sure what I'm doing," I whispered to her as the Mass began. She knew I was only recently back in the church.

"Welcome to the club," she said.

I had written to her asking about my father's boyhood shortly after dedicating *Dutiful Daughters* to his memory. The acknowledgment had broken my silence about his influence and allowed me to admit how little I knew about him and his family. After he died my mother so seldom mentioned him that it was almost as if he had not existed.

Angela hadn't known my father that well, she wrote back. She remembered how much her mother had loved him, and that whenever he came to the farm to visit he always wore a white shirt and tie. She sent photographs. If I were ever in the area I should visit, she said. That spring, after giving a talk in Chicago, I decided to take her up on her offer.

The cathedral provided missalettes for parishioners, and I was grateful for it. But in truth as the Mass progressed I was distracted by the vaulted ceilings, the statues, the huge crucifix, and my acute sense that these walls had been home to my family. I imagined my father and his parents kneeling in these very pews just as I was now.

My cousin had boarded at a convent school and attended a women's Catholic college. Like me, she had basically left home at an early age and never returned. She became a professional woman, married, and raised four children. She was tall and elegant and smart, but my view of her had always been colored by a snapshot of her as a girl in overalls on the farm with her dog. I had envied her childhood.

I did not feel awkward at this Mass. I followed the missalette and rose or stood or knelt without worry. Here, the statues were covered for the Lenten season in purple cloth. Bells rang for the Sanctus. Late Saturday afternoon, the church held only a handful of women and men. No children cried or wandered the aisles. Across from us, an old man prayed the rosary. We stood to say the Our Father, and people folded hands in front of them in the old way, rather than lifting palms upward.

When it was time for the sign of peace, Angela hugged me. "Peace, Jeanie," she said. "I'm so glad you're here."

It was a stunning moment — the embrace, the words, the cathedral. I had not fully known how lonely my journey had

been. The force of the long separation from my family struck
me and dissolved. Though I would find some answers about
my father and begin the search for others as a result of this
visit, it was through this liturgical bond with his niece that I
would gain tangible access to my father's faith.

MY HUSBAND DID NOT LIKE TO LEAVE HOME, and I rarely
traveled with others. I made my own way abroad, and it suited
me. I was not as fussy as most people about proper pillows
and bedding, savory meals, and hot water. I was not much of
a shopper. Traveling alone enabled me to get acquainted with
an ease that didn't occur within a group. And now that I was
a grayhair, many people assumed I needed rescuing and were
even more friendly. I had felt safer in Delhi at midnight than
in Boston after dark.

I had assumed that once in Peoria, I would rent a car, get
directions from my cousin, and make my own discoveries. But
when I saw how effectively and completely Angela had organized my visit I gave myself over to her expert management and
loving care.

We made the forty-mile drive north to Stark County to our
grandparents' farm under gray skies and a dreary drizzle the
next day. Early that morning we attended Mass at her neighborhood church, an angular multi-sided building with its own
charms, however modern. Altar girls dressed in white assisted
the priest. A ruby sanctuary light hung in the sacristy. And
again it was the sign of peace that carried my father's faith
to me through her. Like him, she wore her religion easily and
kindly and completely.

My father's rose-colored headstone was as I had remembered
from the time my aunt brought me to the isolated country

cemetery. I stood before it, shivering in the damp air. I did not
believe in caskets and burial and gravetending, but it was right
to have come here. The tiny plot of land was filled with stones
that bore my name, my father's name. I had already seen that
several of the windows in the village church had been donated
by the family. The continuity was leveling, as if the entire clan
embraced me, as if I had not had to invent myself, as if maybe
I had really come from something, from somebody.

The farmland itself lay loveless and flat and barren several
weeks before planting. We pulled into the site where the barn,
the homestead, and outbuildings had stood. At a great distance,
a single tree broke the line of the horizon. The soil was gray
and dry. The buildings had been razed many years previously,
and all that remained was a towering aluminum silo. I did not
get out of the car, and my cousin and I sat there quietly for a
time, each with her own thoughts.

A year or two before he died, my father and I walked together over the land with the tenant farmer. The two of them
spoke about *al fal fuh* as if the word itself were sacred. Several of the farmer's many children, barefoot and in tattered
clothes, trailed us like reminders of the life I would never lead
and the one from which my father had escaped. One of the
girls chewed a strand of dark hair. The farmhouse still had
a dirt floor. Chickens roamed inside and out. A water pump
stood in the courtyard. I remember that my father picked
up the black earth in his hand and let it fall through his
fingers.

Even then I wished for more than one experience of living.
Farm life must have seemed more authentic to me, with its
smells and animals and fresh air, than the life of manners to
which my parents aspired. I had not been allowed to have a

pet — too dirty — and had been forced to keep my fingernails clean. I hoped that when I grew up I would live here.

In the hundredth year anniversary of my father's birth, nothing was left — not one mark of a foundation or stick of the wooden buildings to indicate that people had once lived here. I remembered the white farmhouse with its blue trim. The wind blew cold. I wondered how the family had spent its winters in this desolate place. There had been cows to milk, of course, and chickens to tend, but the actual growing season was short. The nearest Catholic church had been thirty-five miles away when my father was a boy, and the family sometimes traveled by horse and buggy to Sunday Mass. I had read that visiting priests sometimes said the liturgy in farm houses on the prairie followed by the rosary. It could not have been an easy life.

I had been horrified by the revelry at my father's funeral. People I did not know and relatives I had never met brought pies and lively conversation to the wake. They gathered in the corners of the funeral home and talked about themselves while my father's open coffin lay before them. It was the way country people had of getting together, my mother told me.

Angela and I talked on and on about farm people, though I said nothing to her about the pies at my father's funeral. It was a tricky business: asking about a way of life that was long gone without either romanticizing or looking down on it. We went to village libraries where the staff were only too eager to bring hundred-year-old newspapers from their storage places and to make copies for me. I read about prairie life, learned about the old local feather factory, saw ads for land in Nebraska and articles about the literary societies and Fourth of July picnics.

I was touched by the level of detail my cousin had considered for my visit. She made sure I saw the class photograph of my father hanging in the high school hallway. She had gotten copies of his transcripts from both Spalding Institute and from Saint Viator's College. We had gone to his parents' house in Peoria, and though she was not a person keen on the past, she told me all that she knew. She gave me a copy of the family tree.

When Angela asked about my mother and the reasons she had severed ties with the family, I explained that she believed the family never accepted her because she was not a Catholic. In actual fact, the more I considered it, the more I thought my parents' differences arose because one had been from the city and one from the country. I said nothing about my mother's recent revelations about her abortion. Angela had baked cookies from a recipe she claimed my mother had given to her mother.

IT MAY HAVE BEEN OUR LAST EVENING TOGETHER that she got out the boxes of her mother's old photographs and told me to take what I wanted. Hundreds of sepia-colored snapshots tumbled across our laps and littered the sofa between us, the silent chronicles of family history. Many existed as postcards in the style of the times and had been mailed with one-cent stamps. The faded messages in pencil had come from people we were unable to identify. But there suddenly was my grandfather aiming a rifle at wolves that circled the barn. In sun bonnet and long dress, my grandmother fed her geese. Photographs of my father in overalls as a boy with his dog or his horse made me smile as if he were my own child. Girls and boys of his grammar school, some of them barefoot, posed for an annual picture outside the one-room schoolhouse. And there in what looked like his first suit of store-bought clothes was my father going to high school.

Batches of black and white pictures of my sister and me as children, neatly identified on the backs in my aunt's steady hand, fell from envelopes. Snapshots of my parents on the day of their marriage and on vacations before my father became ill lay before us. A professional photograph of our house in Philadelphia made me wonder if my mother had also sent one of their home in Chicago from which she had told me the story of her unhappiness with my father. If it was there I did not see it.

---

*"She told me to find a nice old priest."*

---

Then as quickly as a wish, I came across the picture of Angela with her dog, the one I remembered so well. The field where she sat appeared newly mown, and I imagined its powerful scent. She wore pony tails and squinted into the sun as the shot was taken. Instead of the overalls I remembered, she had on a checkered dress with short sleeves. "How I wanted a dog," I said. "I wanted your dog."

"Oh, that old thing," she said. "He was some old farm mongrel."

Her girlhood had been no more idyllic than anyone else's, I guessed. She had been an only child. She had had to walk two miles to her one-room country schoolhouse, she told me, and in the winter her father walked ahead of her, making a path through the snowy drifts. There was neither running water nor electricity in the country in those days.

I examined with new regard the high school and college pictures of my cousin when she had become so glamorous. My father had spoken of her endlessly and was as proud of her as he was of my sister and me. She wore long gowns and held gigantic bouquets. The past melted and then faded.

"Mom would be so happy to know you've come back to the church," Angela said. She looked to the ceiling as if heaven and her mother might be right there above us.

We both laughed.

"She was your godmother, you know," she added.

"Oh, I know," I said. "She told me to find a nice old priest."

"She did? She never told me."

"Oh, yes," I said. " 'Not one of those new, young ones, but a nice old priest.' "

"Well, good for her," she said.

"It just took me a little longer than any of us expected."

Though I had come to Peoria to learn about my father, to know something of his boyhood and of his people, the past mattered less and less in any spiritual way. I was still curious. Who had he been? What did he care about? What had he studied? Why did he leave the seminary? But my most compelling question had been answered — the question I had not even articulated to myself. And I knew now that I was irrevocably Catholic.

## ~ 11 ~

# TRIDUUM

O N PALM SUNDAY, just a few days after my return from Peoria, I processed with the others from an upper room at Saint Stephen Priory into the chapel. Waving palms distributed among us by John Allard, we were led by an energetic guitarist through the halls. The event signified Jesus' entry into the city of Jerusalem and the beginning of what used to be called Holy Week. Ordinarily the march might have struck me as childish and artificial, but my time in the Midwest seemed to have made me more tolerant, though I confess the image of the Pied Piper leading the rats out of Hamlin occurred to me. Perhaps if we had started the procession outdoors we would not have needed to follow the musician single-file. I remember wondering if I would ever stop picking at the efforts of the hierarchy to involve the laity in the Mass.

The focus had shifted from an entire week of prayer and reflection on the agony of the crucifixion to the three liturgies of Holy Thursday, Good Friday, and Easter Vigil — called the Triduum. For reasons I don't now recall, I went to another church for the Thursday service instead of to the priory. Perhaps I was rushed. It might have been that the reputation of its choir and a cantor drew me there. The buoyancy from the visit with my cousin made me eager to participate.

The priest who celebrated this Mass would be given a "medical" leave only a few months later. He was a gaunt man with a long, dark beard and very thin face, not unlike that of a *sadhu,* a Hindu holy man. I had seen these emaciated ascetics wandering the streets in India and Nepal in their orange rags, sometimes casting themselves in strange postures for hours at a time. The Holy Thursday priest's eyes burned black with the intensity of his mission. He was well known for casting out the bingo players from the church basement when he arrived in town the way Christ had eliminated the money changers from the temple. The parish had been operating in the black for the first time in decades after he took charge and congregants agreed to the tithing requirement.

Though he must have repeated the words of the liturgy hundreds, maybe even thousands of times, the priest had the wherewithal to make each one new. I couldn't tell how he managed it. Perhaps it was the surety of his own voice rising among us. Usually priests rushed through the Confiteor, swallowing the humbling supplication even before it was uttered, but this time each word was enunciated for us and with us. And while there were some portions of the prayer I might edit out, there were many phrases I loved. The simplicity of the phrase "I have sinned," for example, existed not as a question for me but as a statement about the human condition. The rhythmic acknowledgment of "in my thoughts and in my deeds, in what I have done and what I have failed to do" connected me with that humanness. He paused then — the priest — as if he were waiting for us to enumerate for ourselves whatever shortcomings led us here on this evening to pray with him.

The music did not disappoint me, though this was another congregation that mouthed the lyrics but did not sing. John

Allard thought Catholics' lack of musical participation had something to do with the fact that the religion had been forbidden in Ireland and that people were used to quiet worship in order to stay safe. I thought it more likely that too many hymns were atonal or unfamiliar. It wouldn't kill the church to use "Onward Christian Soldiers" once in a while. The congregation echoed the responsorial psalm in spoken voices. I shuddered. I really hated the responsorial psalm. For one thing, I could never remember the line unless it was sung. For another, the changes from the beautiful language of the King James Version to the modern New American Bible struck me as travesty. If you could change the words in a line of poetry you could alter anything. I took a deep breath and reminded myself why I had come. I thought about the cathedral in Peoria where my family had worshiped. I thought about the Last Supper, the event specially commemorated by this liturgy. The extraordinary color of the da Vinci fresco came to mind.

And then the priest spoke. "Those," he said, "who wish to have their feet washed must sit on an aisle."

At the end of the pew I occupied, two persons away, a woman in her forties removed her shoes and socks. Red polish covered her nails. The priest moved down the aisle with his entourage, kneeling before each "apostle," and slowly, very slowly washed his or her feet. An aide held a basin of water. Two kids carried stacks of white terry cloth towels. How long would the same water be used before replenishing? Was it hot or cold? And who would choose to participate?

Hokum. Pure and simple. Like the handshake of peace I had found so distracting, this foot washing offered only the gimmick of a church trying to keep up with the video age. I may never have known my father well, but I was sure he would never in a million years have gone for this practice. Nor, I imagined, would my cousin. I missed her now and wished I had asked her opinion about the changes in liturgy.

Now the priest approached the pew where I sat. He knelt deliberately before the woman at the end and held her foot for a long time as if it were a wounded animal and he was deciding what to do with it. His fingers were pale and long and slender. Finally he lowered the foot into the basin and gently spread the water across it. The organ played on and on. Though the ritual required only twelve to represent the apostles, anyone who wished to participate could do so. I looked at my watch. Nearly an hour had passed already. The face of the woman showed no expression.

What would be next? Would the parishioners draw straws to see who would actually be crucified as some did in Latin American countries?

I wondered again how the Vatican II people decided what liturgical things should stay, what should go, and which new ones ought to be added without offering some sort of trial period for experimentation and evaluation. The faith required to be a believer presented so few difficulties for me. But reenacting Christ's washing the feet of his apostles at the Last Supper seemed way off-center. It was creepy. I had read that the pope himself kissed the feet of his priests after bathing them.

Christ had not washed the feet of strangers. He went among the people that gathered to hear him preach in order to bring them the word of God. He went to minister to the sick, to heal the wretched, to bless the meek. He invited us to reconsider definitions of the poor. Or was I overreacting again to something harmless that had particular meaning for others?

What did I care so long as I was not required to be part of this equation?

I tended my own mother's feet each time I visited her in Florida. We soaked them in warm water to soften the nails before cutting. The basin I used was not unlike the priest's at the Holy Thursday service. When the water cooled I replaced it. And after a time, I dried her feet with a soft towel and cut the brittle nails she was now unable to reach herself. A person could make a living today traveling from one old person to another with a stool and a pair of clippers. I had seen them in retirement facilities and nursing homes. Two minutes. Snip snip. Fifteen or twenty or even twenty-five dollars a foot. Surgical gloves. No eye contact. Maybe it was not the indignity I thought. Obviously it had nothing whatever to do with this Holy Thursday business, or did it?

Taking care of my mother made me a good daughter perhaps but not a saint. And I had no right now to be so judgmental. But this public display of the bathing of feet did not appear loving. It was grandstanding.

Now all of us were on our knees while the priest circled the church several times praying for our sins. The organ played a dirge. We knelt for so long that my legs ached. I remembered the love command. I remembered that sin was now secondary to forgiveness, to honoring that which is human in all people. I remembered Jim Keenan's admonition not to model ourselves after saints and ascetics. I sat down and rubbed my kneecaps.

What would the Illinois farmers of a hundred years ago have thought of this ritual, those families who bathed once a week if they were lucky? What about the Catholics in third world countries where water was in such short supply? It was this very sort of dissonance with western practices that had taken me to the Himalaya and to other remote cultures. I did not want to participate in a society of affluence that only went through the motions of caring for others. And how was it that the priest washed the feet of women? If we could not be ordained because the apostles were men — that, at least, was the canon law explanation — then it would seem to follow that our feet also would not qualify.

---

*I tended my own mother's feet each time I visited her in Florida.*

---

In my confidence, I once again failed to distinguish between the faith that was firm and strong inside me and the practice that frequently made me so vulnerable. But I think now it was more than that. When placed next to the laity's lack of influence on church policy, the Vatican II changes in the liturgy appeared more and more like so much tap dancing. They were what my father would have called inconsequential.

By coincidence this year, the Boston Marathon had taken place three days before Holy Thursday. I thought about those runners only a few miles out from the starting line who would never catch up. Some were unable to finish. I identified with those diehards. I had huffed and puffed my way into this new Catholicism and had so rarely been able to embrace its liturgical practice that I wondered again how it would end. I had been reading *A Testimonial to Grace* by Avery Dulles, the account of his conversion to Catholicism as a Harvard student. The path to grace was straight, he said, but very long and very steep.

The priest now circled the church several times before kneeling at a side altar for many minutes. I thought of his fingers handling the feet of my neighbor in the pew and of his hollow eyes and cheeks. Months later when I heard that he had left the parish on a leave, I knew it was his own personal suffering we had witnessed that Thursday evening.

The twenty-six-mile marathon had its own religious fervor with its practice and sacrifice and witnessing, its pasta loading before the race. It seemed right that the event took place at the end of Lent and that only a few miles from the end of the race a series of steep inclines and descents known collectively as Heartbreak Hill could shatter even the most prepared person's good intentions.

I myself was never a runner. At the Quaker school, we were required each day to run the cross-country course as a preliminary for athletic practices. Long before marathoning became popular, the anguished faces of my teammates turned me against suffering. I might endure foot blisters on a hard tennis court to win a match, but while others were running the usual trail, I was stuffing as many Peppermint Patties as possible into my face. My irreverence for questionable rules had shown itself in all areas of my life, beginning from an early age. I had been rebellious and difficult. More often, I simply ignored restrictions and went my own way. But in maturity I had learned to speak truth to power, or liked to think so anyway. Such a thing did not seem possible in the Catholic Church.

The marathon route went within a few blocks of our house. That Monday we settled ourselves by the side of the road to wait for the first runners to go by after the wheelchair contingent passed. Finally the elite runners appeared. They came bobbing up and down like a great sea serpent moving down the highway through our town. Everyone cheered. Dogs barked.

Some people held out paper cups of water or orange slices. Thousands of men and women wearing cardboard numbers passed in shorts and T-shirts and running shoes. A few runners wore gloves. A helicopter droned above us. We looked for people we knew. After a while, the crowd thinned. We talked about going home. In front of us a woman sold pretzels from a cart with clear plastic windows. When I bent to look through it to the other side, the bodies of the runners were distorted as if they were dream people. The ordinary folks, those who might take three or four or even five hours to get to the finish line in downtown Boston, arrived. Men with big bellies, women with white hair, determined people with pain etched into their faces struggled to take each step. Some had perfect bodies but awkward gaits. Others walked, holding their sides as if their journey had been too much for them. If the procession into Jerusalem celebrating Palm Sunday was triumphant, the way to the end of the marathon and to Golgotha was fraught with suffering. It seemed both blasphemous and inevitable to set one against the other — the man who suffered for the sins of others side by side with the exercise ethic of western society. I had read in one of Jim Keenan's books that he felt closest to God when he was running. We got home in time to watch the winners of the marathon cross the finish line on television. They wore crowns of olive leaves.

ON EASTER MORNING, I woke with a prayer on my lips. The sun shone. A few dusty pink tulips had bloomed overnight. I was, as usual, awed by the natural world. At the priory, we sang "Morning Has Broken," accompanied by the same guitarist who had led us on Palm Sunday. The aromatic scent of lilies permeated the chapel. Father M., the leader of the anger and forgiveness seminar, celebrated the Mass. As he walked down from the altar for his homily, he spoke without notes about the divinity of all things and of the opportunities for rebirth and renewal, weaving the spiritual and the mundane into something at once ordinary and extraordinary. He seemed genuinely glad to be among us.

During Lent when I was a girl, the Sisters of Mercy taught us to move silently among the Stations of the Cross, contemplating the many sufferings and humiliations of the crucifixion. We learned again and again about the betrayal of Judas and Peter's denial. Even after the resurrection, there was Doubting Thomas to consider, with his fingers in Jesus' wounds. I think we were all glad when the season ended.

On this first Easter after my return to active practice, I had some of that same sentiment. I had not walked the Stations of the Cross. I had not deprived myself of chocolate candy or movies. People over sixty were not required to observe the fasting guidelines and I had made no attempt to follow them. Yet even as the lilies at the priory filled me with hope for the growing season, a weariness crept over me.

Outside the chapel, the sisters I knew from the seminar with Father M. wished me a Happy Easter. We would have two more classes together before they returned to their missions. The Virtue Ethics class at the seminary was also winding down. I tried to remember where I had been on Easter the year before this one, but I could not.

# ~ 12 ~

# PROVINCETOWN

**B**LUE WAS THE COLOR of the Virgin Mary. Robin's egg blue. In the old days, May was her month. Whether she was still honored I had no clue. Post–Vatican II Catholicism seemed to have less and less to say about her. The hierarchy had been concerned about excessive Marian worship. I wondered if that accounted for the disappearance of the rosary and the prayers to the Mother of God after Mass.

Starting at the end of April, we kids had lined up to draw lots to see who would get to crown the Blessed Mother at our school each May morning. The lifesize statue stood right in the second floor landing atop the steep stairs just outside the girls' lavatory. We gathered in the halls and in the stairwell for prayers, after which one of us stepped forward with the crown of May flowers and climbed up the stepladder in order to adorn the Mother of Christ. The month culminated in a procession from the school to the church, where an even larger statue was crowned by an eighth grade girl in a long white gown and veil, the May Queen.

Some of my friends wore medals of the Virgin Mary partially colored with blue enamel. "Mary conceived without sin, pray for us who have recourse to thee." The prayer circled the image in tiny letters. My mother drew the line at my wearing a medal or even a cross around my neck. Occasionally I slipped the rosary I had received as a geography prize over my head.

These were the things I thought about as I settled myself in Provincetown for the month of May the year I returned to the church and found myself surrounded by color. The ocean at the very tip of Cape Cod was dark blue-green, not the robin's egg of the May I was remembering. Still, the purple wisteria that dotted eaves and fields everywhere, the hedges of bridal wreath, and the budding roses evoked those earlier times. Provincetown possessed its own sacred qualities. The combination of sea air and brilliant light perpetuated a kind of fourth dimension not available elsewhere. No wonder so many artists worked here. Both geography and climate encouraged, indeed celebrated, beauty and composition. And the dunes and marsh grass underscored Provincetown's grand isolation.

Some few restaurants and galleries opened a limited number of hours before the summer season. Day visitors might show up mid-morning, having driven from the city, but they were gone by afternoon. I had set aside the time to complete a project I'd been at for nearly a year without the usual interruptions at home. Two rooms on the third floor of an old house on Commercial Street were perfect for my needs. The rear windows had been replaced with a single large pane of glass overlooking the sea. From it, I watched the tides twice each day. I noted the sun and moon and their rising and falling, the seagulls' protest at each change of light. While pigeons strutted gray beneath me on rooftops, I read the Gospel of John and a new book by Philip Roth. I took to the beach and nodded to dogs and their walkers. One was a Great Dane named Gandhi. I got a library card. Mostly I worked.

I had looked forward to attending Mass in Provincetown. In a community of artists, a large percentage of which were gay and lesbian, I had expected a liberal slant. I had expected a significant AIDS ministry. When the pastor played an audio tape of the bishop seeking funds for his annual appeal as a substitute for the homily, I was disappointed. But I was not outraged. What a long way I had come since Ash Wednesday. I went elsewhere.

The hand-carved doors at Our Lady of Lourdes Church in Wellfleet were painted many colors, robin's egg blue among them. From the street they might have depicted an underwater scene. Up close, almost inside the color, it was more difficult to know the artist's intention. I rubbed my palm across one section, and its smoothness told me the story of hard work to achieve the beauty of the sea off-shore like this. I wondered how many hours and days of sanding had been required to raise the grain of the wood before painting and could very nearly hear the rubbing of the paper back and forth. And these were the objects Vatican II wished to eliminate by erecting churches that doubled as gymnasiums?

Inside, the village church was much like those my cousin had shown me in Illinois, small and cozy and personal. Ten or fifteen rows of pews aligned themselves humbly beneath the stained glass. The church was not full but the talk among congregants grew as if something exciting was expected. I saw that a few people had cameras. Some of the women wore gay hats with flowers and pastel-colored suits. I thought of a wedding, but I knew Catholics did not get married on Sunday. For a second my heart fluttered: a May procession?

As a grandfatherly priest entered, he beckoned two children to come forward. The girl wore a white dress with pink sash, the boy dark trousers and a white jacket with a carnation in the lapel. Eager parents and family in their polished shoes and toothy smiles snapped photographs. The kids grinned into the flash bulbs. It was First Communion Sunday.

The priest, obviously delighted to be presiding at the occasion, sat with the youngsters on the altar steps. He did not put his arms around them or speak to them in any diminishing way, declining to treat them as babies. He spoke about what a wonderful day it was for them and for their families and for this church to welcome them into its community as full members. They waved to relatives in back rows and lost whatever small bits of self-consciousness they had brought with them in their new clothes.

---

*The children looked as if the priest was telling them the most fascinating story they had ever heard.*

---

"Now," he said, "let's get down to business." He rose, went to the side of the altar, returning with what looked like a pickle jar, holding it up before the children.

It had already been quiet in the church. Now a hush fell over us as we viewed the white circles inside the inelegant container.

"Do you know what these are?" he said, shaking the jar so that the wafers rattled against its sides.

I don't remember what the children said, or if, in fact, they said anything. The priest continued. "These are the hosts, right?"

The kids nodded.

"These are the hosts we practiced with, right?"

More nodding.

"But they are not yet the body and blood of our lord Jesus Christ, are they?"

The children nodded again but knew quickly from the priest's reaction they were wrong. They stopped.

"Do you remember why they are not yet the body and blood of Our Lord?"

"No," said the girl.

The boy looked away.

"These are just hosts from the bakery," said the priest, "and are regular ordinary bread. You remember tasting them, right? When we practiced?"

Practiced? The kids practiced with hosts?

"But the priest makes the bread and wine holy at Mass, right?" The priest continued his lesson.

The children looked as if he was telling them the most fascinating story they had ever heard, one they had heard many times, one maybe even they could tell themselves were they not so fond of listening to this man.

"And today, for the first time, you two will receive Holy Communion."

Now they nodded gravely.

"But first," he said. "Let me ask you a few questions. Would that be all right?"

They looked at their parents, then at the priest. They were ready.

"Do you know the Our Father?"

They shook their heads.

I wondered what would happen. It didn't seem fair to make the kids do a recitation at seven years old.

"Do you know any of the commandments?" he asked.

Nothing.

"Have you heard of the commandments?"

The little girl removed the pink flower that had been pinned to her hair. The boy dangled his feet from the step.

"I want to tell you a story," he said gently without missing a beat. "Would that be all right?"

I myself nodded.

"Once a long time ago," he said, "when I was in the first grade — and that was a very long time ago — I had a terrible time." He paused. "I couldn't memorize my catechism. I was the same age as the other kids, and I tried my best, but no matter how hard I tried, I just couldn't get it. So when it came time for my first communion, because I had repeated first grade, I was a year older than the others."

I thought of the many personal stories of other priests they had shared from their pulpits — their dental appointments, their cancers, their dead relatives — and how perfectly right it was this time for a priest to share his humanness.

"God loves us no matter what we know or how fast we learn. Did you know that?"

As the priest returned to the altar to finish the liturgy, the children sat with their families. They received the Eucharist. Afterward, on the grass before the church, there were more pictures, this time in front of a white magnolia at its peak. The grayness of its trunk appeared deep and pure and new as a perfect sea creature.

It had been an astonishing performance.

"What a lovely day," a tall, older man in a straw hat said to me. He had a woman on his arm who wore a camera around her neck.

"Don't you just love these kids to pieces?" she said.

I did. I loved the kids to pieces. I loved the day and the occasion and the liturgy. I loved the easy way I was pulled into conversation with the families and the quality of my own joy at witnessing the event. And I especially loved placing it beside the memory of my own first communion. The event in Wellfleet swallowed the time between the two initiations and connected them as tenderly as the magnolia petals in their May blossoming. Perhaps other adults present also looked back to their own inductions. But though I remembered the lace dress and veil I had worn so long ago as certainly as I heard my father coughing from his pew, it was the worry that I wouldn't get my first communion right that came to mind now. The host had attached itself to the roof of my mouth and I wondered what would happen to me if it didn't dissolve. Now the children stood with the priest while cameras clicked. I supposed that the rehearsal with the unconsecrated hosts was not vital. Perhaps it was even inconsequential. But that May morning with the sun's warmth beating on my arms and face like sweet music, the kindness of practice with unsanctified hosts before first communion seemed to me the best new thing about modern Catholicism.

DURING THE REST OF THE MONTH, the moon grew in its fullness. I watched it each evening rise from the sea, the power of light offering a steady reflection on the day. From a wooden table where I sat looking over the day's work, I thought sometimes of the risks of solitude, and I wondered what kind of person would dare to be alone with nothing but her own resources. Yet in the way in which I had often merged so completely with mountains and their inhabitants, I became one with the rhythm of tides.

One afternoon at dusk, the sea flattened out colorless before the sky lost its clouds and the white sun vanished. And
at last the full moon rose pale as a whisper. I had developed
the habit of keeping watch while gulls squawked the end of
day as they gathered and dropped the clams from their beaks
onto rocks, gathered and dropped, again and again until the
shells broke open. On the morning beach, their yellow plastic eyes and mangy feathers made them scavengers. At day's
end, they rode the air currents with elegance and persever-
ance. Night slipped over the wharf, the boats of fishermen,
and closed around the seaside dwellings as a blanket of prayer.

Well after midnight, I woke. Tubes of yellow light beamed
from the moon, beamed without end into the perfect mirror
of the sleeping sea. The cross they formed disquieted me, and
I stood in one place for a long time, feet cold on the bare
floor. If not for my own shivering, I might have imagined
myself a spirit in some ancient drama I could not name but
whose lines I felt desperate to know. Such a spirit might have
knelt before this moon. Did I? I know that I turned away
and came back, turned away and came back. For minutes or
hours, dominating everything, there was nothing else. Then
receding, rising, smaller, hazed over with mist and rings, the
moon passed to the west over the pier, the village. At dawn
even the gulls were silent.

It is not a simple matter to receive such a message from
the sky, to acknowledge the sign of light reflected in me. It
had swooped me up, carried me into the sea's gentle rhythms,
rocking, soothing, holding me in safety and in love. Lives of
prayer can be altered by necessity as well as by choice. Several
of the nuns I had met at the priory in the anger and forgiveness
seminar had related their experiences after Vatican II. Some

had been cloistered and were required to move into the community. The orders of others had been forced to close when
women chose to leave for secular lives. The day after the full
moon reigned over the ocean at Provincetown, I thought of
a sister who had joined a contemplative order after her own
community disbanded. She hadn't known how necessary the
silence was for her, she said, until she found her new group.

Leading a quiet life free from distraction was nearly impossible in the modern world. It was not just the actual noise of
media outlets and highways. It was the constant hawking of
items for sale and the presumption that each of us would be
better were she to own such things. It was the territoriality of
all creatures, the pettiness that arose from dispute, while during all this time the trees grew tall in the forests, bore their
cones, swayed in the wind, provided homes for small animals,
and eventually fell in their time. Harmony could come and
go in a life, as the contemplative sister had so clearly pointed
out to me.

The time without the constancy of human voices freed me
to note the transformation of the dunes after a stormy night.
I had always been confused by abundance, by style, and by
what others deemed valuable. Reducing life to its barest essen-
tials saved me from those awkwardnesses. The monastery in
Bhutan, the missionaries in Bolivia, the interest in mountain
people, and now the weeks of solitude in Provincetown —
these were woven into the uneven experience of my return to
faith by means of the necessary thread of silence.

The tiny town library, just across the street from my rooms,
held unexpected treasures: movie classics on video, dog-eared
volumes by obscure poets, art magazines, and political journals. But I wondered who in Provincetown besides me would

be interested in *Prayers and Meditations,* a slim volume of reflections by Jesuit priest Karl Rahner. "We are all pilgrims on the wearisome roads of our life," he wrote.

> There is always something ahead of us that we have not yet overtaken. When we do catch up with something it immediately becomes an injunction to leave it behind us and to go onward. Every day becomes a beginning. There is no resting place or abiding city. Every answer is a new question. Every good fortune is a new longing. Every victory is only the beginning of a defeat.

Well, maybe. Still, there were those moments between one thing and the next, moments of redemption when a person could be whole and free and good. I had not thought of Jesus Christ and the crucifixion the night of the full moon. Neither the significance nor the problem of suffering had presented itself to me. What I knew afterward was that the race against myself to catch up with modern Catholicism had dissolved, and I could rest.

# ~ 13 ~

# SAINT MATTHAIS SCHOOL

T HE SAINT MATTHAIS SCHOOL had its last day, its last day ever, on the eleventh of June. Driving in my old Honda Civic the previous evening from Boston through Connecticut, New York, New Jersey, and finally Pennsylvania, to Philadelphia, the suburbs, I did not know this. I spoke aloud the poetry I had memorized as a child. I emphasized the "k" sounds of "Wynken, Blynken, and Nod," the silliness of "The Owl and the Pussy Cat," and the mystery of William Blake. I spouted all eight verses of "October's Bright Blue Weather." I recalled the recitations before the class when a child bowed or curtsied before announcing the title and the poet. "With expression," Sister would say. "Enunciate."

An old friend from summer camp days, a beautiful woman not unlike my cousin Angela, invited me to stay with her. She was tall and elegant and had led the life I thought my father would have wanted for me had he lived. Even when we were children she had monogrammed stationery. At camp she had knelt by her cot to say her prayers each night. She still wore the small gold medal of the Virgin Mary with just a hint of blue on it. I had been better at field hockey than at praying. We stayed up late settling the details of our lives within each other's experiences. Hers had taken a sad turn several years before when her husband left her and subsequently died. Now she participated in a prayer group in the next town, she told me, and was a Eucharistic minister. She had been to the shrine in Medjugorje twice. Once, she said, her rosary turned to gold.

When I got to the school, I intended to express my thanks to the Sisters of Mercy for their devotion to children. My appreciation for the rigors of a solid education to those who provided it was long overdue. At this late date, half a century after the fact, my testimony would no doubt have more meaning for me than for them. The mission seemed somehow urgent, as if I had finally realized that I had never said goodbye when I was removed from them. I speculated that it was the First Communion Sunday at Wellfleet that had served as a poignant reminder of their loving care, but I think now that the trip was an inevitable part of my return to the church.

The following morning, I stood alone in the school hallway. The sole of each sandal slid across the concrete as if it had been waxed. This was not the same building in which I had learned to love words and poetry. That old fieldstone monstrosity with eight classrooms, one for each grade, had been torn down and replaced some years ago. I had known that but had not expected cinder blocks and fluorescent lighting.

A crucifix and George Washington hung on adjacent walls. Opposite was a sizable scroll with elegant calligraphy:

> *Let it be known*
> *to all who enter here*
> *that Christ is the reason*
> *for this school.*
> *The unseen*
> *but ever present teacher*
> *in its classes.*
> *The model of its faculty.*
> *The inspiration of its students.*

A boy of about nine in shorts and a white shirt captured me with a polite smile and thick black eyelashes. "Can I help you?"

I followed him to the office, remembering as we walked the question posed to me by Matthew McShane in my first class at the seminary: "Are you a Catholic or what?" It seemed a long time ago.

The sister in charge did not remember that I had called to inquire about visiting. "We're all of us upset," she said. She wore an abbreviated veil and rimless glasses. "The last day. Today is the last day." Her voice softened the meaning of her words. She rose from behind her wooden desk and approached me. "Today the building is still a school. As soon as it is empty, the diocese will rent it out."

"What if I had come a day later? What if I had come too late?" Did I say or only think this? I put my hands in the pockets of my green cotton dress and apologized for the intrusion.

The nun, six inches shorter than I, enfolded me in her arms. "Welcome back," she said. "You are most welcome here."

The head of a man, a priest introducing himself as Father Rodgers, appeared just then at the threshold. His body remained in motion in the hallway. "I'm on my way," he said, as if we were all hurrying to some unknown destination.

"Classes are finished," said Sister. She held my arm, my hand. "There is only the kindergarten graduation about to take place upstairs. If you want to speak with the principal that's where you should go. You are most welcome," she said a second time, ushering me back the way I had come where some children remained, helping to pack books and supplies for distribution to other schools. She asked one of them to escort me to the library. In the stairwell, I recognized an old fiberboard print of the Angel Gabriel on the wall, curved now in its ornate frame. I wondered what happened to the statue of the Virgin Mary, the one we had crowned every May morning just outside the girls' bathroom of our old school. The toilets had regularly rebelled against their nineteenth-century plumbing and sometimes overflowed into the hallway beneath it.

> *The nun, six inches shorter than I, enfolded me in her arms. "Welcome back," she said. "You are most welcome here."*

The library was a double-sized classroom with beige carpeting and nearly empty waist-high shelves. I introduced myself to the kindergarten teacher, a young lay woman who showed me to a child-sized seat without any fuss. "All of the parents were able to come," she said. Father Rodgers hurried to the side of a middle-aged, slightly plump woman I took to be the principal, and the teacher turned on the tape recorder.

Eight children of color marched into the room in jackets and ties or in pastel party dresses to the strains of "Pomp and Circumstance." Each set of hands held a long-stemmed red rose as if it might break. Flashing cameras made stars in the room. Everyone grinned as the children took their seats facing us and the program began. After the teacher reported on the progress of a student, the boy or girl rose and recited a poem. The principal awarded the child a blue ribbon and a hug. Father Rodgers gave the diploma and a handshake. One by one, each walked solemnly to the appropriate set of parents to offer the mother the precious rose. At the end of the exercise, there was a rendition of "New York, New York" with the substitute lyrics of "First Grade, First Grade." All of the adults sniffled. Some wept. One child used her diploma as a spyglass. The priest blew his nose. The principal put an index finger in the corner of an eye to stem the flow. My own eyes were moist. Though this was not the same building and all the people were different, I had really come home.

In the old school, this room would have been the fifth grade where in 1948, David O'Neill's father brought in a television set so that we could watch the inauguration of Harry Truman. It was the same place I got in trouble for saying that everyone was entitled to an equal share of the same goods. In those days when everyone worried about communism, Sister Joseph Marie told us that schools with patriotic names like Thomas Jefferson High School were against the United States government. (In Latin America, she said, parents who named their children Jesus were guilty of mortal sin.) My protests got me sent to the principal with some regularity. We memorized the Declaration of Independence and promised never to enter a Protestant church. Seated at our desks with both feet on the floor, we kept our hands folded. We stood to recite or when an adult entered.

It would be easy to make sport of the Sisters of Mercy and their provincial lives. In Boston, Catholics regularly rail against the rules and punishments they experienced during their school days. For a time when I worked as a mental health professional, Catholicism itself was regarded as pathological by some practitioners. And in the eighties when whispers of sexual abuse by priests first became public, many felt justified in their biases.

As the room where the kindergarten ceremony had taken place cleared, we were all invited to a reception downstairs. The principal, Sister Stella, remained behind to talk with me.

Her green cotton skirt and sweater matched the color of my dress. Her perm curled flat against her head.

"The neighborhood of large houses and high taxes is too expensive for the families of young children," she said. "Those who can afford it send their children to exclusive private schools."

I nodded. I had only briefly noticed the leafy streets of Bala Cynwyd, the well-kept lawns. The town marked the very edge of the Main Line, a series of wealthy bedroom communities and estates stretching as far as King of Prussia.

"As enrollment declined, the only kids left were those brought in by parents across the city line who wanted a better education than Philadelphia schools offered. Most were not Catholic. It didn't matter to us."

I knew that the same thing had happened in Boston after the mandatory school busing fiasco.

"After I close up the school here, I'll return to my first love — inner city schools and minority children," Sister Stella told me. "Saint Matthais is — was — nothing like this when we were in school," she said. "We use reason. And love," she added. "Not rote."

"You mean I memorized all that stuff for nothing?" I said.

She cracked a small smile. "Have you seen the computer room? We just can't keep up with the contracts the public schools get."

I wondered if the children still had daily prayers and catechism.

Yes.

I wondered if they still crowned the May Queen.

Yes.

As Sister headed downstairs, I remembered the slim booklet that had been our Picture Study text, the Catholic version of art history. *The Gleaners* by Millet. The reflected sun on stalks of wheat. The fatigue of peasants. We had been invited to imagine the callused hands of the field workers. Of all the scenes to paint, we had been asked, why did Millet choose common people outdoors? It was true that we had no studio art, no gym, no music, that we ate meals in silence. Perhaps my mother was right that it had been a skewed education. Our academic prizes were prayer cards, rosaries, and small statues.

WHEN I SAID GOODBYE to the nun who had first greeted me, she asked if I remembered the names of my teachers.

I rattled them off as if they were the Beatitudes.

"Marcella is still alive," she said.

She referred to *Sister* Marcella, my teacher for third grade.

"She's over at the convent," she said, "in the health care center. She'd love to see you. Do you have a car?"

I nodded.

"Then you must go there right now," she said. "Marcella is such a grand lady." She wrote the address and the phone number for me on a slip of paper. "Call if you get lost."

I never considered refusing. I knew that once I got in my car I could go anywhere I chose. But as if I were watching myself in a pleasant dream, I drove to Mother McCauley Convent in five minutes. I found the health center and asked for Sister Marcella. Led through a modern, sunny, brick building of many sides, past a star-shaped chapel, past women with canes and walkers, to a simple room with a bed, night table, dresser, and two chairs, I found a tiny woman with white hair straightening her bed.

"Marcella," said my guide. "You have a visitor."

The old woman turned. She wore a blue skirt and sweater the color of hydrangeas. Her face was unwrinkled. "Oh, how lovely, my dear," she said. "Do sit down." Her fingers went from the bed to the night table to the arms of her chair where she landed with a squishing sound on the pillow.

"Down is easy," she said. "It's hard to be graceful when you're old."

I identified myself. And she claimed to remember me. She had taught in many places, she told me. "They made me stop," she said several times. "My last school was in Georgia. They made me stop. I forget things."

"What were your favorite subjects?" I asked.

"Spelling and history." She looked at her hands. "Especially spelling."

"I never once won a spelling bee in your class," I said. "Not once."

"That can't be so," she said. "Who were your other teachers?"

I told her.

"Oh," she said, drawing her words into several syllables. "Perpetua."

I was off-balance with this first name business. *Perpetua*. Sister Perpetua. My first grade teacher.

"If you had Perpetua you learned," she said. She accented each word as if it were part of a march. "She was strict. You learned."

Strict? Maybe the nuns were harsher than I remembered. I didn't remember strictness. I remembered learning the Sign of the Cross. I remembered the colored chalk. In the first grade, we sang a song to learn the numbers to the tune of "Here We Go Round the Mulberry Bush."

"Perpetua and I were novices together," she said. She looked to see if I knew what that meant. "I lost her last year."

"Oh, I'm sorry," I said.

"We were such good friends," she said. "We were just kids together, you know, when we began teaching at St. Matthais. We knew nothing. Every night we'd sit around the kitchen table at the convent, all of us, and try to figure out what to do the next day."

Sister Marcella was so small that if I wanted to pick her up, I imagined that I could do it. Her feet did not reach the floor. "Why did you become a nun?" I said.

"A sister," she said. "A sister."

"Yes," I said, "a sister."

"I had older brothers, you know," she began. I saw that it was the right question, that it was a story she remembered and was eager to tell. She looked at the photograph atop her dresser in the gold frame. "My mother," she said. "She was the most wonderful woman."

I waited. Sister took a sip of water. I wished I had brought her something.

"We lived on the docks, you know, and my mother took in boarders. Only my three brothers got their educations."

I said nothing. She did not mention her father, and I did not ask.

"I always wanted to be a sister," she said. "And it was my only chance."

"Lucky for me that you did," I said.

Sister Marcella went on to tell me about her current activities. "Each of us has a little job," she said. "It's wonderful." She folded her hands across her lap. "We have classes. And the chapel is right here. We have Mass every day."

I was remembering her third grade classroom with the wet wool of its cloak room during the winter months. "Do you think you were very strict?" I said.

"We had to be," she said. Again, she regarded her hands, turning them over.

"A word to the wise..." I said.

"...is sufficient," she finished.

---

*I didn't remember strictness. I remembered learning the Sign of the Cross. I remembered the colored chalk.*

---

Both of us were smiling now. And for the first time Sister Marcella seemed like my old teacher. There was the familiar curve of her nose. She had been known for placing one index finger perpendicular to her lips and uttering the familiar word-to-the-wise remark. The gesture itself became sufficient for us, and after a time, we did it as we entered her classroom the way we crossed ourselves going into church.

"I became a writer because of you and the other sisters," I said. But in the way of elderly people in institutional care as their worlds shrink to what they know, this old lady seemed unable to consider what was beyond her immediate experience.

"I wanted to thank you," I said anyway.

She began to repeat herself then, and I could see she was tired. When I left, she was already dozing.

The chapel centered the building which seemed not as big as when I arrived. I slowed as I passed the room, a plain one with several rows of straight chairs facing a table on a platform. A few occupants sat there now. In the hall a woman so stooped with arthritis her body curved like the letter *C* addressed my feet. "It's a beautiful day, isn't it?"

"Oh, yes, Sister," I said. "It is."

IN AN ALCOVE of the Philadelphia Museum of Art that afternoon, I stood for a time before *The Feast of John the Baptist* by Jules Breton. The text beneath the painting read:

> Since ancient times, peasants have celebrated the longest days of summer with festivities such as this dance around a fire marking the feast of St. John the Baptist on June 24, an important occasion in France.

The painting showed seven barefoot women with fires burning around them. They were slim and graceful and jubilant.

Too sophisticated for our Picture Study book, the painting's color and motion drew me into it. It would be several weeks until the summer solstice, but I felt as celebratory as the women in the picture. Afterward, I asked a stranger to take a photo of me outside the museum. There I am in the green dress, looking down the Benjamin Franklin Parkway, standing triumphantly in the courtyard made famous by Rocky Balboa.

# ~ 14 ~

# HOUSE

L ATE IN THE DAY, as if it were a penance, I drove to my
mother's house, the one I left to go to boarding school
after my father died. Though the hill in front of it had flattened to little more than a slope now under the broad expanse
of maple trees on the street, the place seemed little changed.
No children played outdoors. A contractor's van clogged the
narrow drive.

"The body is only the house for the soul," my mother had
once said. For a woman who disdained religion it seemed an
unusual statement. Perhaps that was why I remembered it.

I circled the block and returned, parking in front of the
house. My fingers curled themselves mightily around the steer-
ing wheel as clips of childhood passed rapidly: the burning
of Mercurochrome on my many skinned knees, the pop of
a war-time balloon bursting on the pavement, yellow jackets
in a jar with blossoms of rhododendron, the imperfection of
cartwheels. And something else: my father's garbled shouts
streaming from an upstairs window — speech therapy after his
latest stroke. What did I expect to achieve by visiting these old
ghosts? Maybe I had come here just to prove that I could. In the
rearview mirror, a middle-aged woman with heavy eyebrows
and a long nose, an adult, a person who drove herself from

Boston to Philadelphia and wrote books, presented herself to me. After all this time, surely nothing here could hurt her.

A Korean man in his thirties wearing a red baseball cap answered the doorbell. "Hello," he said through the screen.

"My parents were the original owners of the house," I told him. "Would it be all right for me to walk in the garden?"

"Sure," he said. "And when you're finished come in and see what I'm doing to the house." His tone was musical, his body slim as a gymnast's.

The property extended a hundred yards in the back. My mother had been a dedicated gardener. Later, she would say it had been her variety of therapy during the many years of my father's illness. Broad-leafed weeds covered the lawn now. Shrubs and trees had been slaughtered, the jagged stubs of their trunks like strange ragtag gravestones. The weeping cherry tree, once so perfectly pink in its delicacy, had rotted.

Inside the house, the contractor apologized for the garden. "The last people rented the place," he said. "The outdoor property became a jungle during their residence, and the inside of the house was filthy."

I imagined garbage reeking in the corners where oak floors now gleamed. The walls, once papered in busy prints, shone white. The contractor was a nephew of the new owner, he told me. He had added space, built new rooms while perfecting his English.

I followed. My shoulder bag swung against me like a nagging reminder of the collection of memories here I could not name.

The same chandelier in the dining room caught the light from the bay window. The new people had not yet moved in, although some of their furniture had arrived. The husband, an economist, taught at the University of Pennsylvania, and there were four children.

Wandering through this house when the place had been stripped, when no one lived here, I became part of its reinvention. Walls had been eliminated, a staircase opened, skylights added. Even if I wanted to, I could not reconstruct my original home, I thought, as I trespassed.

My gentle guide recited the litany of his achievements in the new kitchen — the triple oven, the countertops of special slate, the Belgian faucets. The year before he died, my father and I cooked dinner for my mother in this room that was now gone. She arrived from her job in the city at six o'clock, and more times than not, we had the meal on the table within minutes.

Even at ten years old, I usually sat on my father's lap after school, despite his frailty, and said what I had learned that day. The handsome priest from our parish, Bob Gaffney, occasionally visited. A neighbor, John O'Donnell, brought his own liquor, and when the three of them were together, they listened to whatever sporting event was on the radio. They sat and smoked and cheered. Mr. O'Donnell said what the odds were and made real bets with his bookie. My father and Father Gaffney made "paper" bets and kept track of their "winnings" on a yellow legal pad. My father drank eggnog.

It was only as I traveled upstairs behind my guide and viewed the layout of bedrooms that some other glimmer of my life appeared. A porch off my sister's room that ran the width of the house had become two additional bedrooms and another bath. Seven years older than I, she had been away at college during that time that now seemed so present. In my own room, a large one on a corner at the front of the house, twin beds and dressers occupied the center. A carpet was rolled up by one baseboard. It was the only room in the house that remained unchanged.

"Stay as long as you want," said the contractor. He went off to finish his painting in the new bedrooms and left me at the threshold of my old room. As if daring myself to do it, I entered the room quickly. I opened the door to the ample closet I had once converted into a fort and library. It was full of boxes. When I closed the door, a click marked the action as if it had import. I walked to a window and leaned against its sill. My eyes found the wall where a crucifix had hung over my bed. No mark of its tenure remained.

One night my father and I had turned on the gas oven but forgot to light it. We had several times exploded baking potatoes by insufficiently pricking their thick skins, but we always put a match to the gas. Maybe, I thought now, we had lit the stove and it went out. Maybe it had not been our fault at all.

The night we forgot to turn on the oven, my mother came home from her job and found the two of us unconscious. The fire department arrived, opened the windows, and carried my father and me on stretchers to the front lawn wrapped in blankets. I remember the long jaws of the neighbors who surrounded us and the cold air waking us before anyone did artificial respiration. Now as I occupied the space that had been my old bedroom, I heard the swish-swish of a small brush against the woodwork. My father and I had locked eyes on our adjacent stretchers that night like conspirators.

On most nights my mother tucked me into bed. I was afraid of the dark and needed to be assured she would leave a light on in the hall. One evening soon after the stove incident, she stayed longer than usual.

She had been talking with the family doctor, she told me. "He said it would be easy to put a pillow over Tom's head," she said, "that he would have no strength to fight."

I tried to imagine now the children who would next live in this house, what games they might play, the sounds of their voices. How long would it take them, for example, to figure out that if they jumped hard enough in the center of this room, my room, they could make the dining room chandelier sway?

That night my mother asked me what she should do. I thought she expected me to say that I would smother my father with a pillow. The wooden crucifix given to me on the occasion of my first communion hung over my bed as she spoke of ending my father's life. We had been learning the parts of speech that year, and I parsed her sentences. Mortal sin. Could someone like my mother, not a Catholic, have a mortal sin on her soul if she was not a believer?

"Stay and have tea," the contractor said, after I thanked him for his kindness.

My feet shuffled over the pebbled driveway. My mother had not killed my father with a pillow or with anything else. Several months after the night I have just recounted, a final stroke took him as he lay in a Catholic nursing home. My mother must have been worn out the night she spoke to me about the doctor's suggestion. I had known enough to keep the idea a secret, but the weight of its possibility must have frightened me. I had not fully appreciated its intensity until now.

Driving away at last from the house that had once held the soul of our little family, I tried to remember the name of Lot's wife, though unlike her, I had no urge to look back. Perhaps she had no name.

The house at the end of the street had once been inhabited by a fierce black dog that regularly assailed children with its barking, requiring us to stand quite still until it lost interest and wandered away. As I passed the house, I recalled that the owner had been a tall red-faced man who frequently wore a black sweater with an orange *P* on it. We kids used to say it was "P for piss," though we knew all the time it was for the Ivy-league college in New Jersey. In my relief to be leaving this place, I couldn't stop laughing as I thought of it.

*I tried to remember the name of Lot's wife, though, unlike her, I had no urge to look back. Perhaps she had no name.*

At the top of the hill, I turned left onto a road that zig-zagged east toward the Philadelphia City Line. A placard before the Methodist church now identified it as Vietnamese Christian. My father had driven into the telephone pole just to the side of the church one morning when he delivered me to school. The windshield of the pre-war Packard shattered but we were unharmed. The telephone pole bore the car's green paint for a long time so that it was impossible to pass the place without remembering the accident.

You would think that after this episode and the one with the gas stove, as well as several other close calls, that I would have wanted to stay away from my father. His mood was unpredictable. His physical condition made him unsafe. Yet in the larger sense, he and I were bonded in his struggle together. Everyone knew he had passed out on Philadelphia sidewalks more than once, and the shame of illness prevented my mother from public explanations, so that his shuffling gait and slurred speech were sometimes taken for excessive drink. That someone, the doctor or my mother, would consider getting rid of him had made me his permanent ally. Perhaps I sensed even then that without him the charms and safety of my life with the nuns would be threatened.

I HAD INTUITIVELY SCHEDULED A VISIT to Saint Matthais Church for my last stop. An earnest priest ushered me through the rectory to a side door by the altar. And then, I was alone.

The gold tabernacle door guarded its treasures beneath the eternal flame constant in the same red cut glass. Touching the marble rail where we once knelt to receive the Eucharist, I heard the flow of blood pumping through me, though the moment was less dramatic than I expected. Deep rose carpeting covered the terra cotta floor, but the same oak pews gleamed with high varnish. I circled the edges of the building like an animal marking its territory.

Under our teachers' watchful eyes, we sat with our class each Sunday for the nine o'clock Mass, girls on the left and boys on the right. The nuns' unyielding habits encouraged us to stand taller, to speak clearly, to be on time. The black folds of their clothes hung to the floor and were hauled in by a strap at the waist, extending alongside the rosary beads big as the penny candy we bought at recess. Our hands were clasped in prayer, palms together, right thumb across the left, shoulders back, heads bowed. How reassuring it must have been to know the rules and know that if you followed them you would have eternal life.

Now the darkening colors of stained glass in the Gothic windows blazed their old beauty. I sat in a front pew for some time and considered the Catholic churches I had dared to enter since I had last been here. Soon the night would fall and the day of this reunion would end. From our earliest school days, the sisters had taught us that we were never alone, that God was always with us. I had returned in time to celebrate the mystery of grace. And oh, I was glad. I was just so glad.

*Part III*

# PRACTICE

# ~ 15 ~

# ORDINARY TIME

T HOUGH SUMMER BRINGS THE LONG DAYS we crave throughout the winter, they pass quickly in New England, where the season is brief. On my knees most mornings in the garden, I turned the soil away from its weeds and buried earthworms in their dark places. Even without chemicals, the tomatoes flowered, grew tall, and produced more fruit than usual. Roses bloomed and bloomed again. I began a patch of lavender, and by August its scent filled the yard. Orange Chinese lanterns multiplied in their shady spot. Showy coneflowers competed for space with lemon balm and chives. Sturdy blue thistles blackened with bees. Hydrangeas blossomed full. White yarrow spread into the lawn. Usually the soil was cool on my fingers. I never wore gloves, and it got under my nails and into the pores of my skin.

The eggplant itself seemed especially miraculous when it flowered its delicate hue and then bore fruit. From a three-inch stick with a few shiny leaves it grew into its own sturdy production. I had watched the bud, the blossom, and then the fruit develop from a teardrop into its pear-shaped burgundy yield, twice the size of my hands. Like many vegetables, the eggplant appeared too beautiful to eat. The process of its growth came to symbolize all that was mysterious in my reconversion and rendered a joy beyond anything a human being could achieve.

Summer Masses at the priory occurred quietly without music and began at ten instead of eleven. Without the presence of the sabbatical sisters, the little chapel appeared somehow vacant, and the prior's departure made me sadder than it should have, I think. We had never had a conversation, but his presence had offered a glimmer of what the modern liturgy might become.

By late August, the days closed early. Crisp mornings hung heavy with dew, while monarch butterflies lingered over day-lilies. The Sunday that John Allard celebrated Mass, the priory was only half full. I remember that it had been misting that morning and the grounds sparkled a full palette of green and gold. As the lector read from Ephesians, the sun streamed through the palladium window, over the altar and down the aisle. I had never stayed for coffee, never gotten acquainted with other worshipers, but I was so at home here, so happy.

With few exceptions, lectors swallowed their words. The new liturgy provided only a few lines of scripture, often without context, and by the time I got used to their cadence they were finished. That Sunday, my attention was only partial. When I understood the reading was from Ephesians, I remembered I had been to Ephesus and tried to place it on the map.

"Wives should be subservient to their husbands as to the Lord," read the lector.

No one said anything.

"For the husband is the head of his wife just as Christ is head of the church," the lector said and returned to his seat.

*Subservient. Subservient.*

Father Allard read the gospel. He stepped down into our small congregation onto the Persian carpet to deliver his homily. "Well," he began, "we have something to talk about, don't we?"

Oh, good, I thought. My tutor was not going to let the moment slip by. He would comment on subservience.

And he did. He offered a context. Each person who loved should be subordinate, he said, to the other, male or female, husband or wife. He may even have done a decent job of it, but he did not address the specific writing of Paul's work, nor did he develop the concept of subordination for modern times. I looked for particles of dust on the bare floor by my feet but found nothing.

I wasn't sure about the origins of my fury. Perhaps in the rush to recover whatever portion of my Catholic childhood had been lost, I had turned a blind eye to the conservative church. I had not wanted to get involved in its politics. I had not wanted to think about the gaps in its reform. Perhaps I had hoped to be as I had once been — a little child, safe in ritual and faith, surrounded by religious sisters dedicated to my well-being.

John Allard looked down at the carpet and up again during his homily, as if his notes were written there. The green vestment worn for Ordinary Time appeared too big for him. Occasionally he taught the congregation hymns before the liturgy, and I remembered his perfectly pitched tenor voice. The Mass ended.

"How could you permit the reading of that passage?" I said to him the following week when we met.

He knew exactly which passage I meant. "We do have some discretion," he responded.

"Then why didn't you nix it?" He had given other homilies, fine talks. To be sure, he was no rebel, but the John Allard I knew ought to have a done better job with the reading from Ephesians.

"I just gave it to the lector. He didn't say anything."

"That wasn't his job. It was your job." As I heard the pitch of my voice rise, I thought about the sisters and the anger and forgiveness seminar. Not one of them, I was sure, would ever speak to a priest in the tone I was using.

"I should have checked. But you didn't think I addressed it in the homily?"

"Not well enough." I remember that I said this. I knew I was picking on him. I liked him so much. He had been so kind to me. But it was just this sort of thoughtless adherence to dated attitudes that ate away at the church.

"How could I have given a better explanation?"

"The passage, if it had to be used at all, provided an opportunity to talk about current subservience in the church, differences between men and women. It offered a chance to talk about nonmarital unions. You could have given the group something to take home and think about."

"I'm sorry," he said.

And by then I was also sorry. I had said too much. I knew I could be pedantic and sanctimonious, as if I myself were perfect and knew everything. Most people, probably not even priests, did not go around looking for teachable moments as if they were golden nuggets. But I did not apologize.

"I'm sorry," he said again.

"Isn't this supposed to be the people's church?" I said. "I came close to raising my hand while you were speaking."

A mark of real terror crossed his face. "Oh, God," he said. "Don't do that. This isn't a Quaker meeting. You know that."

And then I did apologize. "I'm sorry," I said. "I wouldn't really raise my hand. I might walk out, but I wouldn't make a scene."

We retreated then to old territory. At Saint Stephen's, individual congregants had the chance to request their own prayers during the liturgy. John and I had a long-standing discussion about these supplications. The individual petitions had a narcissistic quality to them, I thought. When there were people in the world without enough to eat, it hardly seemed right to ask for attention for individuals in suburban Boston. One woman asked for prayers for continued healing for her family every single Sunday.

"Have you ever talked with her?" the priest asked me, "to see what it's all about?"

"No way," I said. "Look. Suppose each person made her own request aloud. How would that be? Would you ever be so personal?"

I don't remember what he said then, but I knew that he would not. Wasn't the bulletin board outside the chapel where notes were regularly posted asking for special prayers good enough? I think now that no matter what the topic I would have been disgruntled. The fact that two thousand years after Christ the Catholic Church had permitted a reading in its parishes about the subordination of women was impossible to ignore. When John said that I was the only one who commented to him, that made it even worse.

At the end of our session that day, when he asked if I thought we could still meet after my response to his homily, I was taken aback. Was he angry with me? No doubt I had come on too strong. Priests were not used to being challenged about their theological interpretations.

"But whom will I ask if I don't have you?" I said.

A person can cross a bridge unaware, even pass through water to another place, leaving her old skin behind, or her house. It's easier to pick at something else than oneself. Had I pushed John Allard beyond what was fair? I hoped I had not.

At home, I took out Joan Chittister's book *In Search of Belief*. I had purchased it after my first Mass, the day the roving eyes of the statue of the Virgin Mary followed me in the little religious shop. The Benedictine nun considers the traditional Apostles' Creed and invites readers to examine faith from a less orthodox, less literal view. After my first reading of the book, I knew that I already shared Chittister's politics, but I believed that I would need to find my own way out from tradition to a more liberal theology. One of the blurbs on the back cover describes the book as "dangerous."

By now, the first of the many subscriptions to Catholic magazines and journals I'd requested were beginning to arrive. These supplemented the reading and the coursework I had done, framing them in a current context. It was reassuring to get away from orthodox positions, to find myself among those who questioned certain practices and theologies. These were serious people who cared about what happened to their church. I read the *National Catholic Reporter* and *America* and *Commonweal* cover to cover. I was forced, at last, to accept the fact that there was no going back — that the church I had known as a child was, despite pressures from the Vatican against it, in the continuing process of reshaping itself. Articles challenging the status quo were progressive and exciting. The writing was thoughtful. But Catholics disagreed in priorities and in patience for change. Perhaps Vatican II's most egregious error had been to ignore the nature of change itself: that it is a process, not an event. It had left people uncertain and angry and afraid of loss without adequate replacement.

Earlier in the summer I had attended a meeting of the Catholic caucus at the National Women's Studies Association conference. Seldom had I been in a group that expressed such confusion and rage. Two women religious — a lamb and a lion — led the discussion. One could not see beyond her own disappointment and anger that only men continued to be permitted to enter the priesthood, while the second sister listened pastorally to the group's concerns. She tried to help them articulate their individual issues, while the first sister repeated all manner of abuses within the church. I came away thinking they were both correct, that both tasks needed attention, and that the battle would be lengthy, with many casualties. A number of the students said they could not remain in the church of their families.

> *I was forced, at last, to accept the fact that there was no going back — that the church I had known as a child was in the continuing process of reshaping itself.*

Anger is often necessary for reform. Sometimes even high drama is required to institute change in complacent organizations. When I first heard those with differing views described as "dissidents," I had laughed out loud. The old-fashioned, paternalistic reactions of the hierarchy were hard to take seriously. Blind authority had surely had its day. But that year when the Vatican issued a new proclamation saying that only those who believed in Christ were eligible for eternal life, I permanently aligned myself with others opposing such views.

I got acquainted with the local chapter of Call to Action, a national organization dedicated to reform. It was a sad group, I thought at first. The unhappiness of its members seemed transformed into cynicism and a sometimes fractured agenda. Most had given up going to traditional liturgies. Some were involved with faith groups that met in people's homes. I was told that priests were present and offered the Eucharist. The liturgy was described as interactive.

I had spent many years lobbying for change within the mental health establishment. I knew what that kind of commitment involved. You had to keep yourself at a constant pitch of imbalance and outrage and focus. I was not prepared to do it again. And I was grateful that there were so many good people both vigilant and dedicated enough to make a difference. But as I regarded the "dissidents," I thought that they needed more centralized leadership. There were groups of married priests seeking their pensions. There were once-married women who sought reparations for annulments. Many nuns hoped for ordination. Homosexuals, the separated and divorced, a few lonely parish priests, Eucharistic ministers — all wanted validation. I wondered who was listening.

THE NEW PRIOR was a handsome, athletic looking man in his forties who had been the chaplain at Providence College. I decided to give him a chance. But at the prayer petitions, he asked the congregation "to bless and to pray for the unborn." Usually when someone said this, I gave no response, a silent protest. And it was, of course, the prior's right to lead his parishioners in church dogma. It was just that it did not tell the whole story. It gave no room for compromise, extenuating circumstances, forgiveness. The petition refused to recognize the fact that Catholics supported a woman's right to choose in the same numbers as the general populace. When the petition continued week after week, I accepted the fact that I would likely need to go to some other place.

I had been in Provincetown on Mother's Day when my daughter called me to announce that she was pregnant with her first child. Since she was in her late thirties, I was not supposed to get too excited, she told me, because the risk of miscarriage was very high. Right. We spoke about decorating the baby's room. The family made lists of names. By summer's end, we had already bought the layette and chosen a crib. Maybe it was because I had been thinking so joyously of babies that the liturgical petition for the unborn seemed exceptionally shrill. An abortion and a live delivery were two sides of the same complicated coin.

When I met with John Allard again in September, he agreed that the tone at the priory had changed. In addition to the prior, several new and conservative Dominican friars were now in residence. Within a year, he would also leave, as would Father M., the instructor of the seminar I had taken with the sisters on sabbatical. I wasn't sure I had the stamina to make another round of local churches to see if I could find a liturgy that didn't offend my sensibilities. John Allard and I had both apologized after the Ephesians wives-be-subservient conversation, which had effectively marked my entry into the Catholic dissident community rather than any major rift between the priest and me.

The days were still briefly warm when the sisters on sabbatical arrived for the fall. I had offered to facilitate a workshop in writing for them, and John had helped to get the seminar into their program.

# ~ 16 ~

# MERTON DAY

THE THOMAS MERTON POETRY RETREAT took place at Saint Stephen Priory on September 23, 2000, the centennial of my father's birth. As I made my way up the lovely drive that had become so welcoming to me, I imagined only a handful of participants. Inside, a hundred chairs were arranged in the large parlor. Most were already taken.

In addition to his famous *Seven Storey Mountain* about his conversion to Catholicism, Thomas Merton had written a number of other books, including poetry. The leader of the retreat, a teacher at the Boston Latin School, was to lecture about the Trappist monk's life in the morning, followed by Mass, lunch, and an afternoon of poetry.

I looked around the room. What was it that drew this many people to spend a Saturday in September indoors? I learned of the existence of an actual Merton Society, which held regular meetings for the purpose of study and discussion. The dark wood paneling and walk-in fireplace held the workshop leader's words in grandeur. From a bay window, light streamed, despite what had turned into a cold, drizzly day. The teacher from Boston Latin School had the mannerism of pausing now and again for emphasis with a professorial hum as he warmed to his topic. His enthusiasm was contagious. I imagined him with a class of his high school seniors and remembered the uninspiring English teachers I'd had at the Quaker school.

In truth, I had not found Merton's poetry compelling. I had come because it seemed important to pause for the occasion of my father's hundred-year anniversary. I would never know his opinion of *The Seven Storey Mountain* or even if he completed the book. But I had wanted to spend the day honoring his memory in some special way.

Our instructor allowed as how he had once considered but ultimately rejected a priestly vocation. Other readers must have been drawn to Merton for that reason: a glimpse into a life that might have been theirs. Many of those present for the workshop had been to the monastery in Kentucky where Merton was ordained and where he had resided.

The popular autobiography had been published in 1947 and was a runaway bestseller. A religious coming of age story, it details his youth in Europe, his return to America, and his conversion to Catholicism. In the sixties, he spent time in Asia, developed an interest in Zen, and wrote much of his poetry. Mysteriously, he was electrocuted to death in Thailand.

The line between an artist's work and his life can be very thin. In some rare instances, the art and the life are one. I knew from *The Seven Storey Mountain* of Merton's youthful indiscretions. He had been a drinker, a party-lover; he had flunked out of Oxford. But these had been self-revelations. When the workshop leader said that one of the new biographies claimed that Merton had actually fathered a child the announcement struck me as gossip. This delving into the life of another had the effect of pathologizing the person, I thought. Public efforts to dissect creativity or beauty served to destroy in order to reinforce social norms. But this group took no satisfaction in this new information. There had been a puzzlement about Merton. He had never been held in particularly high esteem within the church. Neither he nor Dorothy Day, another sinner-convert, would ever be beatified by a pope. Now his followers had an explanation.

A coffee break, additional lecture time, and then a liturgy followed. Not quite half of us attended Mass while the others schmoozed in the hallway. When the prior asked for a volunteer lector, the woman next to me raised her hand. From our discussion before the Mass I knew she was Lutheran.

For all my carping about the liturgy, I just could not stay away. Whatever the irritations, the celebration of the Eucharist still united me with my church. And I had grown to love the chapel at Saint Stephen's. Sometimes when I was waiting for John Allard, I sat there alone, both grateful and surprised to find such comfort and relaxation. The liturgy proceeded. My neighbor walked forward to give her reading and returned. During the consecration, the entire row of women in front of us fell to their knees. Even the Lutheran woman knelt, though I did not. In some churches, parishioners had the option of kneeling or standing while the priest altered the bread and wine. Here, the regulars remained seated. Across from us, others also knelt. At the elevation of the host, one older man, a huge man, said in a stage whisper, "My Lord and My God," the ejaculation we had been taught as youngsters. No one would dare use the word "ejaculation" today, I thought. The Lutheran woman took communion.

After the liturgy we joined others for lunch in the cafeteria. I sat with a group of lay parochial school teachers from a nearby town. They were young, blond, and peppy, and brought to mind the kindergarten teacher at Saint Matthais School who had presided the day of its final graduation.

Father M. approached me in the food line and gave me a hug. He had lost about fifty pounds during the summer and had shed about ten years as well.

He had heard about my writing workshop, he said, and wondered if he could drop in occasionally. He had written poetry at Boston College, he told me.

---

*For all my carping about the liturgy, I just could not stay away.*

---

Though the sisters had already arrived and had attended one week of seminars, the writing workshop was scheduled to begin the second week. I would have to let him know, I said. I would need to see if it would be okay with the sisters.

We visited together for another few minutes. I had talked with the nuns at an orientation meeting, and I waved to some of them now across the dining room. I was fond of Father M., but the workshop would be only for women, I decided.

In the afternoon, copies of a dozen Merton poems were distributed. The message, we were told, was to attend, to listen, to be. I was drowsy after the hot lunch and gentle conversation. When our instructor stated the message, I had perversely stopped listening. My mind went to the spine of the Merton autobiography as it sat on the third shelf of my parents' bookcase, and like a meditation, I fixed memory's eye on the gold title and the black cloth cover. Next to it in a rose binding stood *Peace of Soul*, by Fulton Sheen. The Sheen family owned the farm that abutted the Colgan homestead, and my father had followed the future archbishop to Spalding Institute in Peoria and then to Saint Viator's College. My cousin Angela had shown me photographs of the boys in high school. My father had been dead for several years when the archbishop appeared on television with his expansive cape and deep-set eyes. He had been an ardent anti-communist.

The Quaker school vacations did not mesh with those of my friends at home, and as my mother was working, I spent many hours alone in our house. The House Un-American Activities Committee had already given way to the Army-McCarthy hearings by that time, and I watched them closely on television. Eisenhower was then president, and teachers, as well as government employees, had been required to take loyalty oaths or lose their jobs. I had been so lonely during those school holidays that I had sometimes looked through the yellow pages, unable to name what I needed.

While the discussion of the poetry of Thomas Merton continued into the late afternoon, the light in the room faded. I heard myself sigh. I would never know my father's politics or views on the man who had once been his Illinois neighbor — or on anything else. Could it be that one hundred years after his birth in that house with the dirt floor in the flattest place in the world, and fifty years after his death, I still grieved for him and for myself?

It was not that night or even that week or month, but sometime after the Merton Retreat at the priory that I dreamed of my father for the first time in memory. *I am standing at Mass for the Sign of Peace. It could be in the Saint Matthais Church but I am not sure. I feel his arms around me — bony but powerful. The same gravelly voice issues words from his throat. "Peace be with you, honey," he says. "Peace be with you."*

# ~ 17 ~

# SABBATICAL SISTERS

FIFTEEN SISTERS SHOWED UP the first evening for the writing workshop at the priory. They had been encouraged to try out all the seminars in order to see which suited them. And as they had not brought any of their own work, I provided some poetry and several personal essays for discussion. I brought four memoirs and read the opening paragraph of each. I hoped they would try various forms, I said, including fiction.

We had arranged ourselves in the main parlor, the same large room paneled in dark wood and lined with bookshelves where the Merton Retreat had occurred just a few days earlier. Outside the bay windows of leaded glass, the sun dipped into the glowing horizon just as we gathered to meet, coloring the room pink, now orange.

There was always a moment at the beginning of any class I taught when I regarded the sea of faces before me and wondered what I could possibly say that might meet their expectations. The trust that the sisters placed in me to lead them in this seminar was no greater and no less than other groups, but I was especially eager to offer them something of value. As I explained the workshop format, my hands and feet turned cold and moist. When sweat formed over my upper lip, I thought of Richard Nixon and relaxed. I was not a crook. I was only trying to begin a writing group for nuns at Saint Stephen Priory.

The sisters resembled any other group of middle-aged women with a few minor exceptions: two wore abbreviated head gear, and some had crosses around their necks or religious pins on their lapels. They wore casual clothing — sweat suits, slacks, and walking shoes. A beautiful young Irish sister had the auburn locks and creamy complexion of a movie star. Most had notebooks poised on their knees.

"I hope you don't have anything like *Angela's Ashes* in mind for us, then," one said of Frank McCourt's memoir of a troubled Irish childhood in Limerick.

"A disgrace," said another.

Several nodded.

"I didn't think so," said the Irish sister. "I rather enjoyed it."

I muttered something then about the fact that literature that provoked its readers woke us up, caused us to form new perspectives. It was useful and sometimes exciting to hear others' views. This is what I said.

"But did you read it?"

"Well, yes," I said.

"And?"

It was obvious that sides were already forming — the young and the seasoned sisters. "It was a sad, engaging tale," I said. I tried to turn the discussion back to the nature of the seminar, of what they could expect from me, about the opportunity to express their thoughts and get group feedback. I wasn't sure if I succeeded.

"But will you give us assignments?" they asked.

Perhaps I was wrong in not making the class more structured. These were people used to rules and order, but I was determined to let the women make their own choices. I wondered if any would return the following week.

FOUR SISTERS became my regular students for that fall term: a school librarian from New York; a Maryknoll nun and medical missionary just returned from many years in the Solomon Islands; a teacher of deaf children from the Midwest; and a retired woman from Kentucky, where she was caring for elderly sisters in her order. They were bright, literate, and eager. None had studied writing.

Every Monday evening the sisters greeted me at the front door of the priory. We assembled our little group, pulling the heavy pieces of stuffed furniture close together in the elegant room. Sometimes we got ourselves cups of tea in the nearby kitchenette.

It soon became apparent that the memoirs and personal essays I expected would not be written. The demands of the program were such that the sisters had several seminars every day, weekly spiritual direction, and the opportunity for day and weekend trips in the area. Additionally, they had no immediate access to computers or copy machines, and therefore brought single copies which they read aloud. We listened carefully to the spoken words. We imagined their placement on the page. A writer might read her work several times until it became part of us. In the end, I made copies at home to distribute the following week. The sister from New York, Eleanor, occasionally wrote brief pieces of prose, but the bulk of the output that fall was short verse. Since I had begun as a poet, really as a lover of poetry, I was comfortable with this. But the spiritual dimension of the work intimidated me. It seemed arrogant to offer suggestions for work often so prayerful.

The submissions were offered on tiny slips of scrap paper. At first I thought the writers did not sufficiently value their own words. Later I decided I was being wasteful and began to use both sides of the paper when I did my copying. The sisters took to writing on full sheets. Eventually they petitioned for access to the priory computer and made their own copies.

It was not necessary to give assignments. Sister Ann, the teacher of deaf children, honed her considerable talent with haiku-like images about God and nature. The Maryknoll nun, Sister John Patrick, wrote quatrains that appeared easy but contained astonishing depth. Sister Catherine from Kentucky reflected on the grace of others. She had studied elocution as a child, and whatever she read to us sounded prizeworthy. Sister Eleanor wrote humorous anecdotes about her family, full of wordplay that seemed to come out fully formed, as if she had been shaping it for a long time. When she turned to nature and to birds, she brought a keen observation that she claimed, as a city person, was new to her. The differences in style and in voice blended with their experience to give us so much to consider that our discussions were open-ended. When we talked about the sounds of language and reflected on our early school days where we had first learned to love them, I was once more connected with the charms of my Catholic childhood — and with theirs.

I did not immediately say that I had been away from the church and had returned. But because of the Monday time slot, I often came to the class still exasperated by whatever Sunday liturgy I attended as I again cruised the local churches. I had also begun working part-time that fall at a local hospice, a fact that seems less important to me now than it did at the time. Though what was called a "tranquility fountain" trickled like a small waterfall in the reception area where I answered phones and kept medical records, the job was anything but tranquil. The hour and a half each week with the sisters renewed my own spirit, and I looked forward to it. My daughter's baby was due in January. I hoped I could hold the hospice job until then. I said nothing of these things on Monday evenings, but as we became acquainted, the sisters shared the details of their weekend activities with me. They wondered why they didn't see me Sunday mornings at the Saint Stephen's liturgy. I decided to make another effort to attend Mass there.

I realize now how self-conscious I remained about returning to the church. It had become more than connecting with liturgy. If the details bothered me, it was because they were indicative of something else: some lack of respect I sensed for the laity. When the social workers at the hospice said they did not routinely ask patients about their spiritual needs, I was surprised and said so. They were a dedicated group — the staff at the hospice — but the administrative problems within the agency put everyone on edge. I felt that way about the church sometimes. On Sunday mornings, as I sometimes suffered through the liturgy, the two experiences merged. One of my tasks at the hospice involved tending to the tranquility fountain when its mechanism broke down, which occurred with some regularity.

When the religion editor of the *Boston Globe* put out a call for Catholic views on confession, I agreed to be interviewed. It seemed like perfect timing. I assumed the piece would be a survey and that mine would be one of many opinions on the topic. When we spoke I explained the forty-year gap and my confusion regarding changes in the interim. We had all fabricated sins as children, I said, and now I understood that confession/reconciliation was not even required.

But would I ever go to confession again?

I didn't think so. I suggested that God knew what we did, whether we confessed it or not to a priest. The contemporary church no longer seemed to regard priests as vital intermediaries. A person could confess silently and then meditate on her so-called sins. None of what I said was particularly new or radical.

---

*The piece appeared on the front page of the* **Sunday Globe.** *My phone rang for several days afterward.*

---

What became memorable about the *Globe* interview, however, was that because I was one of several Catholics featured in the piece, the reporter called and said they'd like to have a photograph. I was not enthusiastic but agreed. I had raved about the fine hospitality at the priory that had been so instrumental in my return and arranged to meet the photographer there. When I checked to make sure it would be all right, I did so with the concern of not interrupting whatever programs might be occurring that day.

The prior was worried about publicity, I was told. Cardinal Law might not like it. He was sensitive about the wrong kind of public relations. They would prefer that the photograph be taken elsewhere.

When I relayed this message to the reporter, he said he had just interviewed the cardinal for the article. "The cardinal knows that people have differing views on confession," he said.

I did not think the photography issue had anything to do with confession. The hierarchy probably did not want *Globe* readers knowing it held such an expensive property. Or maybe the cardinal wouldn't have cared. The prior was still new in his job. Perhaps he did not want to call attention to himself. In any event, I considered it a strange way of nurturing a sheep recently returned to the flock.

The picture was taken at my home, which turned out to be much easier for me, though slightly difficult for the photographer. He had hoped for visual aids — a crucifix, a missal, a rosary. A large ceramic pig sat on the bookshelf behind me in the shot.

The piece appeared on the front page of the *Sunday Globe*. My phone rang for several days afterward. Catholic friends called to say that they had also manufactured their sins. Others said they didn't know I had ever been Catholic, or if they did know, didn't know that I had returned to the church. A television crew came to do an interview. Without consciously planning it, I had come out.

The sisters cheered when I arrived for the writing workshop.

I walked into the priory and waved as if I were the queen passing in a limousine.

The day before, one of the new young Dominicans had said Mass there. He was a hefty, handsome man with dark hair and a furrowed brow. His contemptuous remarks about the scourge of abortion had nearly been obscured by the clouds of incense he had released from the censer as he circled the altar. We had opened windows and coughed and snickered.

After the sisters congratulated me on my remarks about reconciliation in the newspaper, they said some of the sisters had asked the prior if they could bring in a Jesuit to say Mass.

I lasted only a few more weeks at the hospice.

# ~ 18 ~

# AUTUMN VOICES

F ROST APPEARED ON THE GLASS one morning before
the occasion of winter. Birds no longer chirped to greet
the dawn that arrived later and later. After the harvest when
the last of the chrysanthemums turned brown, I began to note
small rituals that marked my day. My spirits had dipped after
the failure at the hospice. As I reflected on the experience, I
decided it had not been my housekeeping frustrations with the
tranquility fountain that had rendered me so ineffective. It was
my inability to manage the agency's exquisite respect for the
dying alongside its almost total lack of respect given to those
who worked directly with them. As I witnessed the comings
and goings of the dedicated nurses and home health aides who
attended the terminally ill, the tears they shed when the patients
they had often come to love died, my final days there made me
feel helpless and inadequate.

At home, I lifted the shades every morning one by one,
conscious of each new level of light entering our rooms. The
sound of coffee grounds against the scoop held me in its familiarity. On the stove, water bubbled and boiled. The kettle
whistled. I fed the dog one scoop of Purina. My husband
and I read the newspaper and spoke about the day's schedule.
I checked in with my daughter. Her pregnancy was passing
uneventfully.

Because I had taken the job at the hospice, I had not registered for a course at the seminary that fall, and I missed being there. I read Simone Weil's *Waiting for God*. She was a brilliant writer, I thought, in her articulation of which behaviors were acts of love and which were not. Concurrently, I wandered through *Conjectures of a Guilty Bystander,* a collection of essays by Thomas Merton.

> Solitude has its own special work: a deepening awareness that the world needs. A struggle against alienation. True solitude is deeply aware of the world's needs. It does not hold the world at arm's length.

Both writers stressed the value of the absence of distraction and noise and acquisition and surges for power. Both were more ascetic in their lives than I thought Jim Keenan at the seminary would advocate. When I met with John Allard that fall, we talked about the balance between thought and action. Faith was not the issue, and I had never suffered from an inability to act. It was the matter of right action. I think the experience at the hospice had shaken my confidence. I had hoped to be helpful there.

The sisters' writing gleamed and grew and became my great happiness. In the grand room with its regal armchairs and heavy draperies, with just the hint of organ music filtering in from the chapel, they taught me about living their faith, just as their predecessors had when I was a girl. There was no God-talk, no catechism to memorize, not even any bowing of heads if Jesus' name was used in a poem or a paragraph. It was their acceptance of and love for the amazements of nature and the foibles of humankind that spilled over into our evenings together.

I do not want to give the impression that I believed nuns to be sainted creatures or that I liked all of them without exception. Though I came to know and to enjoy several of the other sisters, the writers and I had more in common than some of the others in the sabbatical program.

Their work heightened my own sensibilities to the designs of fine webs of spiders in corners. I imagined the sea sparkling turquoise at high tide or a goat clattering across a boulder on the side of a mountain. When frost finally covered the earth, I wondered what sounds the roots made as they plunged deeper toward safety for the months to come. We were vessels, I thought, through which these events flowed. Simone Weil spoke of that kind of surrender while taking measure of the will to participate. The imagery of the sisters made us all new.

One evening, as usual before we began to look at the work at hand, we said something of our lives since we had last been together. During the weekend they had participated in an exercise where they were instructed to gather and to carry as many stones and rocks on the property as they could. Some had baskets or bags. Others used their hands and arms. They had carried them throughout an entire day. The next morning, they relieved themselves of one stone at a time, again walking outdoors. Though their exercise may have been designed to deal with the burdens of sins or expectations — I'm not sure — I thought of it then, and later, as the heavy load of disappointment a person can carry to weigh her down. It was not easy to let go, but it was necessary.

The night the sisters told me about the stone walk, I used the image to speak about the choices of words and language in writing. Even a smooth stone, a beautiful one, comforting to the touch, could be too heavy to be set among others. It might call too much attention to itself, obscuring the whole or distorting the context.

LATE IN THE TERM, the sisters' work became powerful in its accumulation, and I collected the writing in a small booklet for them entitled *Autumn Voices*. When I was invited to their end of the term holiday celebration I accepted at once. In other years, December's dark days signaled the end of time's possibility, the reminder of things promised and not completed. Now strong as a pine in one of their poems and vulnerable as the deer I sometimes glimpsed at twilight near the priory, I understood that the fundamental question related to human lives, not to God's love or presence, or to the nature of the Trinity. We came to one another with some given things: the mysteries of stars and the faith that sun will rise. The rest was up to us. A mystic, I had read, knew God by experience. Perhaps that was what my father had meant by his refusal to get mired in details.

LARGE SNOWFLAKES whose varying patterns were almost visible to the naked eye fell throughout the day of the celebration for the sabbatical sisters. By late afternoon, the trees glistened, but some branches fell under the weight of the accumulation. Near the end of the 4:30 Mass, the power failed, as the storm continued to rage.

Aside from the art instructor, I was the only lay person in attendance at the liturgy, which we finished by candlelight. Bouquets of Christmas greens and poinsettias decorated the chapel. The sisters were dressed elegantly in an assortment of bright colors. John Allard sat at the organ in a jacket and tie. The prior's purple vestments made him regal. The nuns did all the readings. A tall woman from Ohio gave the homily, a beautifully crafted talk written for the occasion and delivered from the heart. At the sign of peace, I was touched that each of the women in my workshop made a point to cross the room and offer a hug. Following the Eucharist, a dozen sisters — those who had studied liturgical dancing for the twelve-week period — rose to perform. One of the gifted poets from my class was among them. What a talented woman she was — Sister Ann. Like many of those in the program, she would be moving on to a new job when she went home. I hoped she would find a position worthy of her qualities. Now the women swayed to the music, drifting in a circle with small footsteps, lifting their arms up and out to us. Those who wore full skirts drew them into their movements with understated grace.

I had once taught a course on intentional communities in the sixties when people my age joined communes and generally dropped out. I had never once considered including religious orders, though these clearly were the ones that endured, some of them for centuries, held together by common belief and prayer. From my pew watching the end of the dance, my admiration for these women who had dedicated themselves to the service of God soared. I still could not recite the Apostles' Creed by heart.

Following the Mass, we adjourned to the large parlor, the room of our workshop meetings. An open bar and colorful hors d'oeuvres lined one wall on a buffet table. One of the friars circulated, refilling glasses, a bottle in each hand. Already heady, I took the glass of white wine I was offered. At one end of the room, a floor-to-ceiling Christmas tree sparkled without its electric lights. Most of us held candles. Some people took pictures and flashes went off with almost programmed regularity for a time. The art instructor and her husband waved goodbye.

Sister John Patrick found an armchair, and we leaned into it together. Her blue eyes were keen even in the dim light, framed by the few wisps of white hair that strayed from beneath her veil. She had been in the United States Army during the Second World War, before entering the convent, she told me. She was anxious to get back to the Solomons, where nurses were so necessary. "I think my order wants me to stay here," she said, "near the motherhouse where I can get to know my own sisters." I remembered Sister Marcella in Pennsylvania, also tiny, white-haired, and blue-eyed. The sabbatical nuns had just ended a week's silent retreat. Some approached me saying that they had used the sisters' poems for inspiration.

In the cafeteria, the tables had been shaped into a U and covered with white linen. Priests served the meal, an elegant one of several courses. There was wine and dessert, followed by skits parodying the staff. Small gifts were passed out among us. The sisters received certificates for their participation in the program. Finally we rose and moved about the room in a line clapping and singing a song I had never heard but whose words I seemed to know.

The celebration was much like the end of any season of joy. When it was over and some of the women embraced saying goodbye to one another, there were tears and promises to keep in touch. Many of the nuns would be returning after the holidays for the next term, but from my group only Sister Eleanor would be back. The electricity was still off as the evening closed.

AT YEAR'S END, I reflected on the previous months. More than
a year had passed since I had returned from Bolivia, driven by
the outrage of what I had witnessed there to the course on
moral theology at the Jesuit seminary. I had visited churches,
participated in liturgies, traveled. I remembered Jim Keenan's
admonition against complacency. I had grown in the patient
counsel of John Allard. I had faced the old ghosts of my family
and declared my sorrow for my father aloud. Peace and seren-
ity, of course, resided within. It had become a matter of some
amusement for me that the tranquility fountain at the hospice
required so much attention. Nevertheless, it was my association with women of faith, those who had delivered themselves
to something beyond their own individual endeavors, that so-
lidified my commitment to Catholicism. They had made me
strong when I was young, and their willingness to let me share
my strengths with them during these recent months brought
me through the challenge of my old loneliness to fullness.

# ~ 19 ~

# ABUNDANCE

**M**Y DAUGHTER GAVE BIRTH to a baby girl in January on the day of my mother's ninety-third birthday. The new session for the sisters on renewal got underway, and another group began the writing workshop. I registered to audit a course on Ethics and the New Testament at the Jesuit seminary. The snow arrived and covered us for weeks, splendid as fine memories, insulating us from excess noise. The scotch broom that lined our driveway froze to ice and glittered in a constant strobe.

When John Allard told me he would be leaving in the fall in order to teach full time at Providence College, I was delighted for him. The priory was too small a world, I thought, to contain his intellectual gifts. But I would miss him. He had anchored me throughout my ups and downs in the new church, providing information and support. As I had come to know him, I realized what real luck it had been that we were well-matched in our basic sensibilities. He continued to help me with questions about practice and to press me about the nature of faith, not just in general but in my life as I lived it. Occasionally his remarks jarred me with their boldness, like the one about my having something in common with Jesus. I admired his willingness to take me on. Now with the prospect

of John's departure from the priory, combined with its frequently boilerplate liturgies, I blessed myself with holy water
in the vestibules of new churches and hoped for the best.

It turned out that the sabbatical sisters themselves had been
trying out other churches in the area. After all, they said, they
were in Boston for such a short time. They wanted to take in all
they could. There was no reason to sit through disappointing
liturgies, they told me.

"Sometimes I'm just so angry after Mass," I told them.

"We, none of us, are happy with it, Jean," said one of the
new writers, a peppy woman from Dublin who spoke with less
of a brogue than we expected.

"Really?" I said. Her remark startled me. I must have
thought my dismay with the modern ritual had been my failure
to adjust to it. I realize now that I regarded it as some cruel
initiation I was unable to pass, rather than the fault of those
empowered to give it meaning. The sister from Ireland was
young, a bike rider, a secondary school principal. It was not
her nature to mince words.

Saint Paul's Church in Wellesley more nearly approximated
my childhood parish community than any other I had yet visited. Those who participated looked like people I may have
known from other places. They were healthy, well-dressed,
and athletic. They were white. A few older parishioners wore
mink coats. In addition, the liturgy was held together by the
voices of an exceptional choir. One of the priests serving
the parish had himself grown up in Wellesley and returned.
Tall and wholesome looking, he loped through his duties
like a pole vaulter, accepting and giving love like a favored
son. The church even had an elementary school. Tow-headed
children accompanied their parents to early Masses. In the

parish bulletin, I read that a book club met regularly in the rectory.

But the sisters kept talking about Saint Ignatius Church on the Boston College campus. The homilies were exceptional, they said.

The church was only half full the first time I went there. On Commonwealth Avenue in Chestnut Hill, its Gothic arches and steeple were actually dwarfed by the college's library several blocks away, which from the outside appeared more cathedral-like. Trying Boston College out as a graduate school possibility, I had taken a course there in the pre–Doug Flutie days when the campus was less crowded. The instructor, a layman, had required us to stand by our seats before each class and say the Hail Mary.

*The sister from Ireland was young, a bike rider, a secondary school principal. It was not her nature to mince words.*

The stained glass at Saint Ignatius, the stone interior, the wooden altarpiece with cross were not the things I noticed that first day I attended Mass. The choir and music, full of modern chords and halftones more like Copland than Bach, alternately soothed and challenged the ear. The sisters had warned me that the congregation did not sing, refused to sing. The priest delivered his homily as he walked up and down the aisle and spoke of "the Vatican II miracle," which, I confess, eluded me. It was his happiness to be there, much like Father M.'s at the priory, that I found so engaging as he spoke about the gathering of adults in this place.

Behind me, a person of questionable gender in a watch cap slumped in a pew. At the priory and at the church in Wellesley, parishioners regularly left their jackets and purses on their seats when they went to receive the Eucharist. I knew such a thing did not regularly occur here. When I turned to shake hands for the sign of peace, I saw that the watch-cap person was a woman with many plastic bags at her feet. She waved a tiny salute to me instead of touching hands, and I was somehow grateful that she asked nothing, except the right to be here on a cold Sunday morning. The pews surrounding us were empty, and I had to reach two rows ahead to find another hand for peace.

I did nothing about the homeless woman that day, though I wondered if I ought to mention it to the priest on leaving the church. It was a hard thing to know the right thing to do. Should I have asked the woman if she needed something or would that have been an intrusion? These were old questions for me, and I had no new answers to them. During the next months I would see the watch-cap woman again, and others like her, at Saint Ignatius. I would come no closer to knowing what if anything I should do to let them know they were not invisible, but I knew I belonged among them.

In the 1940s, we pried both ends off the cans that held our soup and string beans. I had been allowed then to step on the containers, squashing them flat for the war effort. We rolled old aluminum foil into balls. When the nuns examined the remains of our plates, we understood that the crusts of bread would be of great value to others and we did not create waste. After the war, there were clothing drives for refugees. And while to my memory we did not see photographs of either Holocaust survivors or of other postwar Europeans, the first book we were required to read at the Quaker school was *Hiroshima* by

John Hersey. None of us there needed pictures to imagine the Japanese homeless who survived the atomic bomb.

It was an odd contrast — my situation of privilege and abundance with the palpable awareness of others' lives — though one common, I think, for many westerners. I was sure now that I had gone to the Himalaya and returned again to take in the confident abundance of faith I found there in an effort to compensate for the spiritual poverty in which I lived in America.

In the Ethics and New Testament course that semester at the seminary, there was frequent commentary about Christ's "preferential option for the poor." I was just beginning to read about the liberation theology formulated by Latin American clergy in response to economic poverty. The course was taught as a seminar by Jim Keenan and another Jesuit priest. The perspectives of third world students peppered discussions. Men and women from Gambia, the Philippines, Indonesia, Germany, France, and Great Britain sat at the conference table, as well as those from the States. Nearly fifty were enrolled in the course as seminarians, graduate students, auditors, or visiting ministers. Many were already ordained priests. A handful worked as administrators in local parishes or on boards of Catholic organizations. Their knowledge and commitment and the skillful leadership of the seminar made me believe the church might actually be in good hands.

Discussions were lively and respectful, though often heated. It was remarkable, however, one afternoon in the middle of a class when a student flung up his hands and shouted, "Stop. Just stop." He was one of the older men in the course, returning to develop a second career. He conducted himself with the assurance of a man with many successes, and I imagined he had been an executive in a large corporation, though he was without arrogance.

"Stop," he said again, as the room quieted.

Those at the elongated table paused mid-sentence, mid-thought, mid-gesture to regard him. A woman from Harvard Divinity School held a bottle of Poland Spring water inches from her mouth. The few auditors who sat behind the others looked up from their yellow tablets as I did, waiting.

"I've had it," the man said. "Do you people have any idea how many millions of dollars of property held by the Boston archdiocese" — he paused then so that we could prepare ourselves for what he intended to say — "isn't even" — another pause — "occupied?"

No one answered his question.

"I give up," he said. He went on to say then that there was no real church, that it was so disorganized in its finances and in its beliefs that a person couldn't tell where he was. You could go to any Catholic church on a Sunday morning, he said, and find liturgies so totally disparate that you had to ask yourself what kind of thing you were a part of and where it was going.

Of course, he was not going to give up. At least I didn't think so. He was exasperated. He had gone to a "major" Catholic charitable organization, he said, to see how he could help, only to discover how truly disorganized and unwieldy it was. There were people in need, people right in Boston living on the streets. Catholic schools had to close because the archdiocese could no longer support them, and here, he said, was all this property in idleness.

I was glad for his outburst, as I suspected others were also glad. But no one responded to him that day. After a silence and a few neutral remarks, the discussion continued as if his remarks had not even happened. I spoke to him before the next class and said I was grateful for his comments. He was still frustrated, I thought, but apologetic. The eye of the needle and the bank account of the church — it was hard to know how to shape a reasonable response to them.

# ~ 20 ~

# MUCH TO DARE

MID-WINTER, THE SECOND SEASON of my revival as a Catholic, I enrolled in a Poetry and Prayer weekend at the Campion Retreat Center in a suburb west of Boston. On the original site of the Weston Jesuit School of Theology, its main building was perched atop a hill and surrounded by woods. Pillars outside the main entrance and a rotunda that centered the building seemed slightly at odds with the New England countryside. Even the stone chapel with its high ceiling and stained glass appeared to have been transplanted from some other time and place. The cracked ceiling testified to its age and wear, but it was nonetheless beautiful in the manner of its ancient style.

Because I lived nearby, I was able to commute to the center for the weekend program. The schedule called for talks on poetry several times during the day and evening, as well as liturgy, with pauses for rest and reflection. I was assigned a room in an upper floor dormitory for my needs. Though the room was too ample in size to be called a cubicle, its single bed, the one chair and table brought to mind its other inhabitants, those studying for the priesthood. As I stood at the second floor window of my temporary quarters, I saw no one on the icy grounds. The radiator clanged softly. The wings of several floors were currently in use for the care of sick and elderly priests. I thought Cambridge was a much better place for seminarians than the isolation here.

A dozen people took part in the weekend led by two semi-retired Jesuit priests. We celebrated the liturgy in the same room where we discussed language, merging poetry and prayer and creating our own small community within the monastic setting. Some of us took our meals together in the cafeteria. For these days, the words of the Mass had a particularly fine sound, even in English. Perhaps it was because we were, for that time, a group united in our purpose. The ordinariness of the room and makeshift altar, the music during the liturgy, added by remote control — these facilitated a focus rather than the distraction I had frequently found so irritating in other settings. The lack of pretension, the celebration of the sacred in the everyday gave me one more inkling of what it might be like to be one with the modern celebration of the Eucharist without reservation.

Shortly after arriving for the weekend, I discovered a small loft tucked away behind a third-floor entry to the old chapel. Dark as it was quiet, I had to feel my way to a wooden chair as if I had come late to a movie and my eyes were not yet ready to address the situation. When I sat, my knees touched the railing and I placed my hands over its smoothness. The place felt damp and cloying. But as I stood to leave, the lights came up dimly from the chapel below as from a great distance. The sensation was not unlike a sunrise in the Himalaya when a person could often awake to find herself above the clouds.

I loved the Himalaya. I loved its light and people and the certainty of its spirituality. I loved the lives lived according to the season. There was more: I loved its definition of community that included all. As I looked down now on the empty chapel at the Campion Center, I wondered if I would ever find that among Catholics in America.

I had continued to visit churches, assessing their politics and liturgies and orthodoxy. I had returned to Saint Ignatius and to the church in Wellesley, as well as to the priory. At a church in Cambridge, I circled the place several times before finding an open door. Maybe I would turn out to be an itinerant Catholic. I supposed there was no finish line to faith. The purity of childhood Catholicism, when just saying "Our Lord" made a youngster feel safe, was no longer available. The faith of my father, with or without its details of consequence, was also gone. Since I had begun to reconsider active practice and was more attuned to the subject of religion, I had heard our current era defined as post-Christian. I didn't know what that meant. A two-thousand-year-old message was not one to be given lightly away. I kept the snide joke about showing up too late to the party to myself, but I wondered if the uncertainties of Eucharistic celebrations and the rigid pronouncements about church dogma might eventually break something fine and honest inside me, some continuing hope for this homecoming.

I did not go back to the little third-floor loft. For the remainder of the weekend, I read and reread the poetry the leaders had distributed among us. Sometimes I walked the grounds, enjoying the chill of the air in my lungs and the bumps of frozen earth beneath my boots. I lay on the narrow bed, surprisingly comfortable, and took in the silence and occasional rustlings in the hall. Several other groups had also gathered here for the weekend.

The carpeted room designated for our use must have been part of a renovation or recent addition. Its walls were smooth.

The lighting beamed indirectly from the ceiling. We listened carefully to the words of modern poets and marveled at their use of language to make something so clean, so new. The sisters in my seminar at Saint Stephen's would have reveled in the experience here, and I wished they sat among us. Their bold images had created a winter I had never before seen — one stark and beautiful and prayerful.

SISTER ELEANOR O'DOHERTY had been the mainstay of the writers at the priory. At the beginning of the second term, she recruited two others so that we could continue the group. Their energy and gifts paralleled that of the women in the fall seminar, and I continued to look forward to our evenings together.

One evening during Lent, Eleanor arrived uncharacteristically late. It was unlike her or any of the sisters who were early almost to a fault. We were meeting now in one of the smaller parlors, and I remember that when we closed the heavy sliding doors against intrusion, one of them stuck on its casting.

"I'll go first," she said.

We all looked at her then. The writers took turns reading their work, and Eleanor usually went last by her own choice. We placed our mugs of tea on the glass table without a sound alongside the pages of writing and waited.

"I'm sorry," she said. "I did the best I could. I wanted to bring something."

I thought women apologized entirely too often. I remember that I said something like that as Eleanor took out a single sheet of paper. The computer-generated letters *G-O-D* were printed diagonally and took up the entire page in bold print.

I found the sharing of her expression particularly brave. It was no small thing to know the difference between foreground and background in a life, however you lived it. Perhaps because I had so infrequently named those things that had touched me most deeply, I failed to recognize their presence.

*That evening with the sisters I was held in safety and comfort by the power of belief.*

Many of the sisters had visited the Boston art museums. An Edvard Munch exhibit at Boston College had sparked an earlier discussion about the nature of artistic statement. The evening Sister Eleanor presented us with her GOD page offered us another opportunity. We did not speak of her intention. Nor did any of us share our personal reactions. We attempted to regard the work as a statement of being and entered into it on its own terms. Though we had many less serious hours than that one — moments when the sisters reminisced about their days as novices, read poems about children and family, the pleasures of work — I was particularly awed that evening by the totality of their endeavor.

Shortly after this time, my husband would be diagnosed with an aggressive lymphoma, the United States would be attacked by terrorists, and the ugly secret of sexual abuse in the church would be exposed. In the struggle to come to terms with these challenges, my focus on personal faith would recede.

But that evening with the sisters, before it seemed certain that everything would be irrevocably changed, I was held in safety and comfort by the power of belief. Spring was on the way then. The black-brownness of old snow folded away under azure skies. Broken twigs, the news of last November's oak leaves appeared by the side of the road. Boxwood and broomstick shrugged the ice from their shoulders and rose up green again. I remember that I imagined the patter of birds in Tennessee and Virginia, and the shadows of high-flying geese across my shoulders. I knew what it was like to wait beneath the sod for warmer days, for certain blooming. I shook sleep from my skin as if it were the earth itself and prayed myself into warmer days, breath by breath, embracing the passion that claimed me. Sometimes the sun poured in like sand. I was well prepared, I thought, to discover how much there was to dare.

## About the Author

Jean Colgan Gould, a widely published writer, is the author of *Divorcing Your Grandmother* (Wm. Morrow). A regional leader of creative essay and poetry workshops, she lives in Natick, Massachusetts. Her work has appeared in *Sojourners* (where she served as editor of the Women's Forum), the *National Catholic Reporter,* and dozens of other venues. Gould holds an M.A. in Counseling Psychology from Tufts University and a B.S. in Psychology, *summa cum laude,* from Springfield College in Massachusetts. She has also edited two anthologies, *Season of Adventure: Women over Fifty and the Outdoors* and *Dutiful Daughters: Caring for Our Parents as They Grow Old.*

# WOMEN IN THE CHURCH

**Elizabeth A. Johnson, editor**
**THE CHURCH WOMEN WANT**
**Catholic Women in Dialogue**

(Sponsored by the National Pastoral Life Center in New York)

Edited by prominent theologian Beth Johnson, this book is a no-holds- barred discussion among Catholic women about the face of the church, the need for reform and change, and the challenges faithful women face. Contributors include Miriam Therese Winter, Diana Hayes, Elizabeth Johnson, Susan Muto, and Colleen Griffith.

0-8245-1979-5, $16.95 paperback

**Miriam Therese Winter**
**OUT OF THE DEPTHS**
*The Story of Ludmila Javorova, Roman Catholic Priest*

"We need not theorize any longer about what women priests might do for the church. Miriam Therese Winter shows us Ludmila Javorova in action, ministering to the people of God in ways that few men could, as a clandestine priest in the underground Church of Czechoslovakia. This profoundly Catholic book has a bonus: a stunning portrait of a bishop with guts, Felix Davidek, Ludmila's mentor and the man who ordained her, despite opposition from the faint of heart. Davidek is a model of what a people's bishop could become in the twenty-first century." — Robert Blair Kaiser, contributing editor, *Newsweek*

0-8245-1889-6, $19.95 hardcover

Also available in Spanish
*Desde lo hondo*
0-8245-1975-2, $19.95 paperback

crossroad

## INSPIRATIONAL CATHOLIC MEMOIRS
## FROM CROSSROAD

**Steve Kissing**
**RUNNING FROM THE DEVIL**
*A Memoir of a Boy Possessed*

A "hilarious" book (*Publisher's Weekly, Library Journal*), *Running from the Devil* is the poignant and bestselling memoir of one boy's struggle to make sense of his Catholic faith while he believed he was being possessed by the devil.

0-8245-2105-6, $22.95 hardcover


**Deal Hudson**
**An American Conversion**
*One Man's Discovery of Beauty and Truth in Times of Crisis*

*Crisis* magazine publisher, syndicated radio host, and frequent guest on national media, Hudson offers his memoir of the beauty and truth of the Catholic faith as seen through the eyes of one of today's most prominent converts.

0-8245-2126-9, $22.95 hardcover


Please support your local bookstore,
or call 1-800-707-0670 for Customer Service.

For a free catalog, write us at

THE CROSSROAD PUBLISHING COMPANY
481 Eighth Avenue, Suite 1550
New York, NY 10001

Visit our website at
*www.crossroadpublishing.com*
All prices subject to change.

crossroad